...ition

Information Technology Key Skills

Intermediate and Advanced Level GNVQ

Glyn Paton
and
P.K. McBride

BUTTERWORTH
HEINEMANN

Butterworth-Heinemann
Linacre House, Jordan Hill, Oxford OX2 8DP
A division of Reed Educational and Professional Publishing Ltd

℞   A member of the Reed Elsevier plc group

OXFORD   BOSTON   JOHANNESBURG
MELBOURNE   NEW DELHI   SINGAPORE

First published 1997

British Library Cataloguing in Publication Data
A catalogue record for this book is available from the British Library

ISBN 0 7506 3378 6

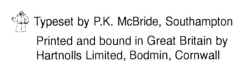 Typeset by P.K. McBride, Southampton
    Printed and bound in Great Britain by
    Hartnolls Limited, Bodmin, Cornwall

Contents

Aims of this Book

> ➤ Translate GNVQ-speak into easily understandable statements that relate to specific IT skills and tasks.

> ➤ Signpost portfolio building opportunities.

> ➤ Clearly show which skills are being demonstrated at each stage.

> ➤ Tell you what type of evidence (e.g. printout, disk file or observation) you should be producing at each stage.

> ➤ Take you step by step through evidence gathering and portfolio building, so that at the end you will have a complete IT Key Skills Portfolio.

> ➤ Relate your evidence to elements, performance criteria and range statements.

> ➤ Show you "How To" in the second section of the book which details how to make the software packages perform all the tasks required.

> ➤ Provide you with a project that is interesting, informative, enjoyable and (if you play cards right) could lead to a good day out.

Using this Book

Your GNVQ Project

The aim is to provide a project around which you can develop and demonstrate your IT skills.

This project is based around the organisation of a day trip, which should be relevant to your course. The trip could be to a gallery, an exhibition, a museum, an industrial or commercial organisation or anywhere that you feel would be an interesting, informative and enjoyable day out. The trip must in some way complement and be relevant to your main area of study.

Here is a brief outline of the way that the project will produce evidence of your IT skills.

Word processing and graphics

A poster to advertise the trip and letters to provide information and updates to those going on the trip.

Spreadsheets and graphics

To calculate the expenditure for the trip and compare costs of different transport.

Database

To store information about those going on the trip. To search for students, sort them into groups and keep their records updated.

General IT skills

These will be needed throughout the project and include skills like file handling, use of directories, backups and dealing with equipment faults.

Project evaluation

As in all GNVQ assessments there needs to be a review and evaluation of your methods and approach to the project.

The Portfolio Builder

The key to using this book and completing your IT portfolio is the **Portfolio Builder** icon or symbol in the left hand margin. The Portfolio Builder icon acts as a signpost to tell you:

➢   *Stages* at which you should be producing evidence for your portfolio.

➢   The *type of evidence* that should be produced. This is shown by symbols within the Portfolio Builder icon. Evidence will usually be in the form of printouts, disk files, or lecturer observation.

➢   The *reference number*, for the Tracking Table.

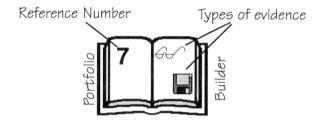

Reference number

The Portfolio Builder reference number is important as it provides the link to the Tracking Table. There is one at the end of each chapter. The tables are vital as they provide full details about the evidence that you should be producing as well cross-referencing to the GNVQ IT Key Skills Standards.

Types of evidence

Types of evidence include:

✍   Data collection

💾   Disk file

👓   Observation

🖨   Printout

📄   Report

Tracking Tables

There is a Tracking Table at the end of each chapter. These tables list all the Portfolio Builder icons in that chapter identified by their reference numbers. The Tracking Table relates each Portfolio Builder icon to the Key Skills Standards and provides full details of:

➤ which elements are covered

➤ which performance criteria are covered

➤ which range statements are covered

➤ the nature of the evidence that should be produced for that given Portfolio Builder icon.

Part of the Tracking Table from Chapter 3 is shown below.

Tracking Table: Word Processing

Ref. No. = Portfolio Builder Reference Number
El. No. = Element Number **PC** = Performance Criteria

Ref. No.	El. No.	PC	Range	Type of Evidence
📖 1	2.1	2	Information; Enter; Software	Early stages in poster design, printouts.
	3.1	2	Information; Enter; Software	
📖 2	2.2	2, 4	Information; Software Edit Reorganising	Printout of formatted poster design, text only.
	3.2	2, 4	Information; Software Edit Reorganising	
📖 3	2.2	6	Combine	Formatted final poster design, with imported clipart, placed and sized.
	3.2	6	Combine	

There are some fairly technical terms or "GNVQ-speak" in this table. Terms such as *Element Number*, *Performance Critcria* and *Range* are very important for assessors and verifiers of your portfolio, and it is essential that your evidence can be linked or tracked to these. In fact you may be asked to write these details (as obtained from the Tracking Table) on each piece of evidence.

Performance criteria and range

In the tables, *Range* is usually referred to by the initial letter in the range description from the Standards. Range descriptions are separated by semi-colons. Occasionally to help clarification an extra word or two is added, in this case the words are linked by full stops, e.g. *Combine...same type*.

You will note that the same PCs and Range are often covered more than once. There are reasons for this; often a Performance Criteria and or Range statement may be complex and require a variety of different types of evidence to be produced for full coverage; also evidence of certain skills may need to be produced more than once.

Levels 2 and 3, Intermediate and Advanced

This book covers both Intermediate (Level 2) and Advanced (Level 3) Key IT Skills.

Level 3 tasks are shown on a shaded background.

Intermediate Key IT

Cover all the tasks *except* those marked Level 3.

Advanced Key IT

Cover all the tasks *including* those marked Level 3.

Building a Portfolio

The evidence for your IT Key Skills portfolio can come from a variety of sources. As long as it is related to your area of study, any work you produce on a computer can be a possible source of evidence. It is likely that you will produce IT evidence as part of your main GNVQ assessment programme – include or cross-reference this as part of your IT portfolio.

If you build your portfolio using the travel project, you will automatically cover these skills. If you decide to do a different project, remember that your portfolio must contain evidence for **all** the skills outlined in the IT Key Skills Check List.

You may produce IT evidence at college, at home or at work (during work experience or if you have a part-time job). If you think an item is relevant, ask the appropriate lecturer to look at the document or other evidence.

However you produce the evidence, your completed portfolio must demonstrate the full set of IT Key Skills. These are described in plain English in the IT Key Skills Check List (see pages 6 – 8).

Use this check list as a guide to portfolio building.

IT Key Skills Check List

General IT skills

Enter info	Enter information correctly.
Error check	Check for errors as data is input and correct accordingly.
Correct faults	Correct and record any simple faults in IT equipment.
Report faults	Report and record any more complex errors or faults that occur.
Use Help	Use on-line help and manuals to assist you in learning applications packages.
Printout	Produce regular printouts to show all stages in document production and design.
Combine	Combine information of same type, but different files.
Cross-combine	Combine information from two different packages, resolving any differences in format and ensuring that they form a well-laid out and coherent end product.
Presentation	Present documents in different forms showing different styles, formats and layout demonstrating that you have sought to obtain the best presentation in terms of clarity, layout and format with a view to fitness for purpose.
Safety	Explain the importance of working safely in line with good working practices.
Remote data	**Level 3. Access remote database to obtain information.**
Save to disk	Save work regularly, particularly after large and/or important changes.
Backup	Make backups.
Name files	Name files correctly and sensibly, with a name that indicates content
	Level 3. Filenames should include a reference to version number.
Directories	Create and use directories.
Close	Close down packages correctly.
Find files	Find files with particular names.

Information skills

Gather data	Locate and gather appropriate information for the task.
Save raw data	Retain this source information (raw data).

Word processing skills

Edit text	Edit documents; including the following operations on text:
	    insert
	    delete
	    cut and paste
	    copy and paste
	    format in terms of layout, font type and size.

Import	Import, place and size graphics appropriately.
Automate	**Level 3. Use of automated routines, e.g. macros and autotext.**
Headers/footers	**Level 3. Use of headers and footers to give date and page numbers.**
Templates (WP)	**Level 3 only. Create and use document template or stylesheet.**

Spreadsheet skills

Design sheet	Design spreadsheet with clear lay out.
Move and copy	Move and copy cells.
Format sheet	Reformat spreadsheet, changing column width and formatting numbers to decimal places.
Numbers	Handle integers and reals. (Integers are whole numbers with no decimal places, e.g. 6, 17, 301. Reals or real numbers are those with decimals, e.g. 1.5, 20.78, 3.143.)
Restructure	Insert and delete columns or rows.
Graphs	Draw a graph from the data.
Cell references	**Level 3. Absolute and relative cell references.**
Templates (SS)	**Level 3. Use and design of spreadsheet template.**

Database skills

Edit data	Edit the database performing the following operations on records:
	add/append
	delete
	modify.
Search	Search on specified criteria.
Sort	Sort records.
Design database	**Level 3. Design a database structure.**

Project evaluation

Finally, as in all GNVQ assessments there is a project evaluation. Your evaluation must include these key features:

Choice of package	Justify choice of packages, explain their use.
Facilities	Describe facilities of the package(s) and relate to overall task.
Alternatives	Contrast use of a package with:
	(a) an alternative choice
	(b) manual non-IT method.
Problems?	Explain any problems when using IT.
IT/non-IT	Compare IT and non-IT processes.
Comparison	**Level 3. Write a report evaluating three examples of information management/processing comparing the manual (non-IT) and IT methods.**
Effect of IT	**Level 3. Evaluate effect of IT on individuals and organisations.**

Information Gathering and Handling 1

Planning your Project

The planning and organisation of the trip will be the way that you produce your IT Key Skills portfolio. Each stage of the preparation for the event will require the use of different packages and different IT skills. Remember though that "IT Key Skills" covers things other than pure IT, e.g. information gathering, project review and evaluation.

Take care over your choice of a place to visit, make it one that really interests you as well as being relevant to the course. This will make the whole process enjoyable. Who knows, if you do this project well enough it could lead to an excellent day out of college, as well as a complete IT Key Skills Portfolio!

The table on the next page describes each stage and the skills area covered.

You will see that the first item on the list is not really a skill, but it is the most important step of all as without it your project will never get off the ground.

For the rest of this book the visit will be based upon a GNVQ Advanced Science group going to the Natural History Museum (London).

You must choose your own day out and replace the information given in the examples with details for your own excursion.

Stage of Project	Skill Areas
Decide where to go	Making your mind up!
Gather information about costs of trip	Information gathering and handling
Throughout all IT parts of the project	*General IT skills. Covering many housekeeping skills e.g. files, directories (see Key Skills list)*
Publicise the event	Word processing Graphics handling
Provide more details to those interested	Word processing Graphics in documents
Calculating costs	Spreadsheet handling and design
Keeping and updating records of students going on the trip	Database handling
Investigating a further trip to Europe	Word processing Spreadsheet skills, including graphing Importing packages
Evaluation of the Project and of IT	Project evaluation Review of IT Health and safety issues
	Level 3. Evaluation of effect of IT on individuals and organisations

Portfolio Building Starts Here!

Transport costs: Investigate and collect data

It's make your mind up time! If you haven't already, you must now make the decision and finalise the destination.

Now you need to investigate different ways of getting there; coach, mini-bus, train or any suitable alternative, and find the prices for each.

In some ways this could be the trickiest part of the whole project. You will need to find out the costs associated with your planned trip, and this may not always be easy. Train prices will be simple to find but you may need to ask an appropriate lecturer to find you a range of coach prices. Remember coaches come in different sizes and prices and at this stage you do not know how many are going and so cannot decide on the coach size, but do not worry about this yet. Try to get as much information as you can. Here is a list of information sources that could provide you with transport details:

➢   telephone (Yellow Pages)

➢   papers and magazines (leisure and travel sections)

➢   Teletext (Ceefax has lots of leisure and travel details)

➢   travel agents.

Always talk to your lecturer before you ask a commercial operation, i.e. travel agent or coach company, about prices. It may be that half of the college may have already enquired about prices and they may be getting a bit jaded!

Travel will not be the only outlay, there may well be other expenses. Here is a list of possible other costs that you may have to include in your budget:

➢   entrance fee

➢   coach parking

➢   other transport (e.g. underground)

➢   food and drink.

Once you have collected all the information on the details above **keep it**, it forms part of your portfolio on information gathering.

Transport costs: Select the best

It should now be a relatively simple exercise to weed out those methods of transport which are clearly more expensive than the other options. This leaves you with the task of selecting what looks to be best three or four ways of getting there. Shortly you will use a spreadsheet to do a detailed analysis on costs, and compare your chosen methods, but now it is time to publicise the event.

Tracking Table: Information Gathering and Handling

Ref. No. = Portfolio Builder Reference Number
El. No. = Element Number **PC** = Performance Criteria

Ref. No.	El. No.	PC	Range	Type of Evidence
📖 1	2.1	1	Select; Information;	Information on prices and different modes of transport.
	3.1	1	Select; Information;	
📖 2	2.1	1, 3	Select; Information;	Selected information on prices to determine best method of transport.
	3.1	1, 3	Select; Information;	

General IT Skills

2

This section covers the general IT skills sometimes called *housekeeping*. Throughout all your work on this project these basic IT skills must be used and demonstrated. You need to be aware of these at all stages and produce evidence that shows that you have these important *day-to-day* IT skills.

Filenames

There are rules you *must* obey when giving files names, otherwise the computer will reject them. There are rules you *should* obey concerning filenames, as these will help you remember what is in the file and the reason you created it.

Rules you must obey

These rules apply to MS-DOS and Windows 3.1. Windows 95 sets no restrictions on filenames.

Can have no more than eight characters, with a three character extension.

Can use only letters, numbers and the symbols _ ^ $ - ! % &.

Must not contain: spaces, backslashes, asterisks, commas or full stops (except the full stop that separates the main name from the extension).

Rules you should obey

Files names should be sensible and indicate their content. For instance one of the first tasks you will do is produce a poster to advertise your trip.

A sensible name would be: **tr-pstr1.doc.** This name tells you the following;

tr   to do with the trip

pstr it's a poster

1   version 1 (important for level 3)

.doc this tells you that it is a WORD word processing file. The package automatically puts this on the end. It does this so that it can find its own files.

Avoid filenames that do not tell you anything about the file contents or that are just plain silly.

Here are some examples that you should **avoid**:

> GARY1 GARY2 GARY3
>
> MONDAY1 THURS2
>
> splat tdctcd blur

A week or so after you created and named them you would have no idea what these files contained.

Directories

A disk drive (where you save your files) can be thought of as a large filing cabinet. Such a cabinet without draws or subsections would be difficult to manage especially if there are lots of files. Disk drives can be divided into subsections by the use of directories. Most people keep different types of work in different directories, i.e. they use directories to classify their work. You should create a directory for your core IT work. This will allow you to easily identify and access work relevant to this project. You may even want to divide this core IT directory into sub-directories, one for each section of the project.

Saving your Work

You may have heard that computers never make mistakes, but they are prone to failure. Loss of power and a faulty disk drive are two relatively common and potentially disastrous problems that can occur. Either of these could cause loss of work with great inconvenience. However, simple measures (saving and backing up) can be taken to ensure that there is little or no loss of data should any of these problems occur.

Saving your work regularly

Imagine you have spent an hour on the computer designing a poster to advertise your trip. Suddenly and without warning there is a power cut. If you have been saving your work regularly there will little or no problem, but if you haven't, all your work will be lost! Make sure you save every 15 minutes or so, but more regularly if you are making large changes to the file.

Backing Up

This means making a copy of all your files onto either a separate floppy disk or a different directory or drive. This ensures that if some disaster befalls all your work, accidental erasure or corruption, you will have a copy of your work that can be used to "restore" all your files and so only cause a mild inconvenience rather than a complete disaster. Back up all substantial new work at the end of the session.

Data Input, Checking for and Correcting Errors

It is very easy to mistype an entry, hence it is an important part of good computer practice to check that what you have typed in is correct. This mainly has to be done visually, and is especially important for numbers as many keying-in errors cannot be detected without cross-checking. This is not the case for words where a typing error usually makes a nonsense of the word. You also have a tool to help you to detect these, a spell checker. Use a spell checker regularly on all your word processed files. There is no excuse for mis-spelled words in the era of modern word processing.

Printouts

Printouts are your main source of evidence for your portfolio. Therefore it is essential that:

➢ there are plenty of them (see below)

➢ they are clearly labelled

➢ their labels reference them to a particular skill set or part of your portfolio.

Throughout all parts of this project you should make regular printouts. These should occur at key stages in a document's development. For example, in the word processing sections you should always print out the first rough draft, label it as such, make all necessary corrections and modifications, printout and label again. There may then be a final version when you have adjusted the layout and design so that the whole document is now as you want it. Again label, reference and file this in the appropriate section of your portfolio.

On-Line Help and Manuals

On-line help has been a feature of computer packages for a long time. In modern packages, on-line help is a user-friendly and effective way of learning the facilities on offer.

Computer packages are increasingly learned on a "self-teach" basis. This is partly a reflection on the speed of change in the computer world and partly because it is often the best way to learn these things. Self-teaching using on-line help and manuals allows you to move at your own pace and direct your study to an area that you want to learn. This has become so important, that this now been classified as a core skill. So during this project as you learn new aspects of the computer packages make sure you use on-line help and manuals and that you are recorded by your lecturer as doing so.

Equipment Errors

These cover hardware and software errors. Simply, you need to keep a basic error log of all the faults and errors you encounter when using IT. There are two appropriate types of action you may take:

(1) a *simple error*, correct it yourself.

Examples of errors you can fix yourself are:

➢ printer off-line

➢ floppy disk in drive on boot-up

➢ floppy disk not in drive when saving or loading

➢ screen adjustment needs altering

➢ clearing a print manager problem.

(2) a *more complex error*, report to the lecturer and or technician.

Whichever type of fault it is, record it in your error log. This should record:

➢ what the error was

➢ the date it occurred

➢ whether you lost any data

➢ the action you took concerning the fault.

Tracking Table: General IT Skills

Ref. No. = Portfolio Builder Reference Number
El. No. = Element Number **PC** = Performance Criteria

Ref. No.	El. No.	PC	Range	Type of Evidence
📖 1	2.1	4	Store input... ...files;	Appropriate filenames given.
	3.1	4	Store input... ...files;	
📖 2	2.1	4	Store input... ...directories;	Appropriate directory structure created.
	3.1	4	Store input... ...directories;	
📖 3	2.2	5	Appropriate intervals;	Regular saving of files, especially after important changes. Observed.
	3.2	5	Appropriate intervals;	
📖 4	2.3	5	Information;	Backups taken of important files.
	3.3	6	Information;	
📖 5	2.1	2	Enter...accurately	Information entered correctly, mistakes noted and corrected.
	3.1	2	Enter...accurately	
📖 6	All	Many	Many	Enough printouts to show all stages in document production.
📖 7	2.1	2	Enter...manuals and on-line help;	Observed use of manuals and on-line help.
	3.1	2	Enter...manuals and on-line help;	
📖 8	2.1	2	Enter...errors;	Errors dealt with appropriately; reported or fixed.
	3.1	2	Enter...errors;	
	2.4	4	Problems;	Error/Fault log is kept.
	3.4	5	Problems;	

Word Processing

3

Publicity for the trip

In this section you are going to design and produce a poster to advertise the trip and create a letter to give interested students further details.

The Poster

Design a simple poster to publicise your trip.

By creating this poster you will provide evidence for importing, copying, and changing the format of text.

The aim is to enter all the text first and then edit and reformat it so that it looks like a poster.

First draft

The basic text for your poster will be similar to that shown below, but modified to your own trip.

DAY TRIP
TO
NATURAL HISTORY MUSEUM
LONDON

Organised by
GNVQ Science

19 June
Leave College at 8.00 am back by 6.30

Cost around £15

Interested? Contact Shaine, Tracey etc.

Run your word processing package and type this in with details modified to your scheme. *Do not do any formatting yet.*

The text should be displayed at normal size, with no special effects, and lined up to the left of the page (left justified).

Print it out and write "First draft" on the printout.

Save the file with a suitable name.

> **Level 3. The filename must contain a reference to the version number, e.g. *tr-post1.doc*.**

Formatting the poster

By using the following techniques you can transform the plain text into an eye-catching poster as shown opposite.

Changing font size

Changing font type

Centring text

Adding a border and shading

Emboldening text

Importing graphics

Positioning and sizing graphics

You will need to experiment with different font types and sizes as well as the graphics, i.e. what type, where on the page, what size?

How To:

Set fonts and styles
Page 85
Add borders
Page 90
Import graphics
Page 98

Clip art should be available as part of your word processing package and there ought to be a large variety of images to choose from. Importing clipart is quite easy and will considerably add to the impact of the poster. Choose a suitable image and place it in an appropriate position.

Print out a copy of the finished poster, and of any versions of your poster that you reject in the process of getting a good layout/design.

Label your printouts clearly.

If you want to produce a larger, i.e. A3, poster, you will either need access to an A3 printer or you could use a photocopier to increase A4 to A3 size.

> **Level 3. Save each version of the document with an appropriate filename, including its version number, e.g. *tr-post2.doc, tr-post3.doc*.**

DAY TRIP

Increase font size

Centre justify
all text

TO

NATURAL HISTORY

MUSEUM

Change font type

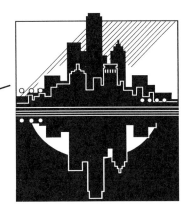

Import a graphic

Add a border

LONDON

Organised by
GNVQ Science Group

Larger, bold text

19 June

Leave College at 8.00 am back by 6.30

Cost around £15

Interested?
Contact Shaine, Tracey or Sue
at the Union Office

Change font

Get a Life – Get Organised

The Letter

The next document to be produced will be a letter to all students who are eligible for the trip giving them further details of the day and inviting them to reply whether they are interested or not.

Later you will edit and improve this letter. This will provide evidence of a wide variety of word processing skills.

First draft

Start a new file and type in a letter to fellow students based on the one below. Make it relevant to your event.

Dear Student

We are planning to go on a trip to the Natural History Museum, London. It will take one day. We need to leave college at 9.00 am and return by 6.30.

We are planning to travel by coach to London and then take the tube to North Kensington. The entrance fee to the Museum is £4.00, the tube is £2.50 and estimated coach fare £8, so the overall cost for the day will be around £15.

Bring a packed lunch.

Bill Evans and Sue Walker be will the lecturers coming along.

The aim of the trip is increase our breadth of scientific knowledge.

Hope you can make it.

Save this document with a suitable filename.

> **Level 3. Make sure that the file name includes the version number (in this case 1).**

Print out the letter and label the printout showing clearly that this is draft number one.

Second draft

How To:

Set fonts and styles
Page 85

This letter is a bit dull and needs be made more interesting. Load the version 1 letter and edit the text and format it along the lines of the illustration below.

Centre justify headings

DAY TRIP

NATURAL HISTORY MUSEUM

Change font

Dear Student

We are organising a day trip to the Natural History Museum, London. We plan to leave college at 8.30 am and return by 6.30.

The aim of the trip is increase our breadth of scientific knowledge.

Travel will be by coach to London and then the underground to North Kensington. The entrance fee to the Museum is £4.00, the tube is £2.50 and *estimated* coach fare £8.00, so the overall cost for the day will be around £15.00.

Two lecturers will be coming along.

Bold and italic

Bold and centred

Hope you can make it.

Save this document with an appropriate new filename.

Print this out and label the printout showing clearly that this is draft number two.

How To:

Import graphics
Page 98

The letter is a lot better now but you may decide to import some graphics here too. Not only will it make the letter more eye-catching but by carefully choosing which graphics to add you can start giving all the letters and posters produced for this project a similar feel or style. This is called a *"house style"*, and it helps the reader to immediately identify the style and layout with your project. Save and print (use appropriate filenames and label the printout).

Importing files — the reply slip

Portfolio 6 Builder

You need to know who is interested in going on this trip. To gather information you will need an extra page which asks for details of interested students. You can include this page with the letter. This extra page is a reply slip that interested students must complete and return.

Later on you will merge this with the main letter, but first it must be created as a separate file.

Your "reply slip" document will look something like this:

Day Trip
to
Natural History Museum

Reply Slip

I am interested in going on this trip. Please send me further details and provisionally book me a place.

Name: ....

Course: ....

Tutor: ....

Please delete as appropriate.

I enclose a deposit of £5.
I will give a deposit of £5 within one week.

Signed: ....

How To:

Merge files
Page 102

Type this in with changes relevant to your trip, check for errors and save the file with an appropriate name. Print and label this and close the file.

You are now going to merge this file into your main letter and edit it so that it becomes a tear-off reply slip at the bottom.

Open your main letter document and follow the procedures in the "How To" section.

Edit this so that it all fits onto one page, you will need to get rid of some headings and spaces. You will end up with a letter similar to that below. When you are happy with the layout, check for errors, save the file with a new name, print it out and label the printout appropriately.

Final draft

DAY TRIP
NATURAL HISTORY MUSEUM
Dear Student

We are organising a day trip to the Natural History Museum, London. We plan to leave college at 8.30 am and return by 6.30.

The aim of the trip is to increase our breadth of scientific knowledge.

We will travel by coach to London and then take the underground to North Kensington. The entrance fee to the Museum is £4.00, the tube is £2.50 and *estimated* coach fare £8.00, so the overall cost for the day will be around £15.00.

Two lecturers will be coming along.

Hope you can make it.

Line of ''s inserted*

****

Reply Slip

Header text deleted — *Bold and centred*

I am interested in going on this trip. Please send me further details and provisionally book me a place.

Name: .... Course: ....

Tutor: ....

Course: line moved

Please delete as appropriate.
I enclose a deposit of £5.
I will give a deposit of £5 within one week.

Signed: ....

Templates and Stylesheets (Level 3)

Portfolio 8 Builder

To organise this trip properly there will need to be several more letters to students. These letters will:

➢ provide students with further details and exact costs

➢ enable you to gather more details about those going. For example, you will need to know student's address, age, sex, course and state of payments.

These letters should be instantly recognisable, they should be distinctive (as mentioned earlier they should have a house style). You can use templates or stylesheets to help you do this. All you need to do is open a new file, and decide the following:

➢ the font to use as standard

➢ the size of the font

➢ the standard layout, e.g. margins and justification

➢ whether there will be a standard heading.

Possibly your file may look like this:

GNVQ Science

DAY TRIP NATURAL HISTORY MUSEUM
19 JUNE

Information to those going:

Text will go here

....

....

How To:

Create templates
Page 88

Having designed this you simply save it as a template. Then whenever you want to send letters concerning the trip you simply select this template and it will automatically provide you with the same layout for all your letters.

Once you have designed the template, and saved it as a template print it out and label it.

Automated Routines (Level 3)

Portfolio

9

Builder

Both macros and autotext are features on word processing packages that automate processes and can save you a lot of key strokes and/or mouse operations. You can use either one of these to demonstrate the use of automated routines.

Autotext

How To:

Use Easy Text
Page 92

Autotext (known as Easy Text in Works) simply allows you to replace a commonly used word with a simple set of mouse clicks to save you time and keying-in. For example, in the previous letters (and future ones) commonly typed in sections of text would be **"GNVQ Advanced Science"**. You can define this bit of text as autotext and never have to type it in again! Another likely candidate could be **"Day trip to the Natural History Museum"**.

Decide on the items of text that you want to make "autotext". Define them and include them in future correspondence.

Macros

How To:

Use Help
Pages 71 – 80

These are more sophisticated as you can use these to store commands as well as key strokes. For example, if you wanted to go through some text emboldening and underlining sections, you could use a macro it to do automatically (on a given key combination) to any highlighted text.

All word processors operate autotext and macros in slightly different ways, and how to use these features is described in the "How To" section, but this is an ideal opportunity to use on-line help and manuals to show you how to use one of these automated functions.

Using on-line help and automating with either macros or autotext are Key Skills that must be observed. You will need to demonstrate them to a lecturer so that he or she can document your use of these features.

Tracking Table: Word Processing

Ref. No. = Portfolio Builder Reference Number
El. No. = Element Number **PC** = Performance Criteria

Ref. No.	El. No.	PC	Range	Type of Evidence
📖 1	2.1	2	Information; Enter; Software;	Early stages in poster design, printouts.
	3.1	2	Information; Enter; Software;	
📖 2	2.2	2, 4	Information; Software; Edit; Reorganising;	Printout of formatted poster design, text only.
	3.2	2, 4	Information; Software; Edit; Reorganising;	
📖 3	2.2	6	Combine;	Formatted final poster design, with imported clipart, placed and sized.
	3.2	6	Combine;	
				File names with version numbers incorporated. (Level 3)
📖 5	2.1	2	Information; Enter; Software; Store;	Printouts of all stages during letter production. File saved at appropriate intervals during production.
	3.1	2	Information; Enter; Software; Store;	
	2.2	2, 4, 5	Information; Edit; Reorganise; Appropriate intervals	
	3.2	2, 4, 5	Information; Edit; Reorganise; Appropriate intervals	
📖 6	2.2	6	Combine...same type;	Combined/merged word processing files to produce letter with reply slip.
	3.2	6	Combine...same type;	
📖 7	2.3	4	Requirements... ..consistent;	Final letter has recognisable style and consistent format.
	3.3	5	Requirements... ..consistent	
📖 8	3.1	5	Configure software;	**Use of templates or stylesheets to produce documents. (Level 3)**
📖 9	3.2	7	Software;	**Use of automated routines in a word processing package. (Level 3)**

Spreadsheets 4

Introduction

You will use spreadsheets on this project in order to:

➢ calculate the overall cost of the trip

➢ determine how much each student will have to pay.

The advantage of using spreadsheets is that it allows you to make these types of calculations very easily, and with a bit of care, present the results clearly.

Spreadsheet Concepts

If you have never used spreadsheets before then you should read this section, otherwise skip to "**Calculating the Costs**".

This part aims to give you an overview of spreadsheets – what they are and what they can do. If you are completely new to spreadsheets, ask your lecturer for some trial exercises before you tackle the spreadsheet tasks for your portfolio.

A spreadsheet is divided into grids or cells. Each cell has an address, made up of its column letter and row number. Hence the very top left-hand corner cell is A1, one down is A2 and to its right is B2.

You can move the cursor to any cell and place data in there.

Types of data

Formulae and functions are the key to the flexibility and capability of spreadsheets.

Spreadsheets recognise four types of data:

Labels, or text, are used to give titles and headings.

Numbers, numeric data upon which calculations are performed.

Formulae tell the spreadsheet what calculations to do. Most – but not all – calculations are mathematical. Formulae always start with either an "=" or a "+" sign:

e.g. =B4+C4

this says add the contents of these two cells together.

Functions can be written into formulae to handle more complex mathematical, financial and other operations:

e.g. =AVG(C4...G4)

This formulae uses the function AVG() to find the AVeraGe of all the numbers contained in the line of cells from C4 to G4.

The example below shows simple calculations from a series of social events at college. It includes all these data types. Note that when you type in a formula you normally see the numeric result of that formula and not what you actually typed in. In the top view, the sheet has been set to show the formulae and functions as they were entered. Below, the sheet has been set to show the results.

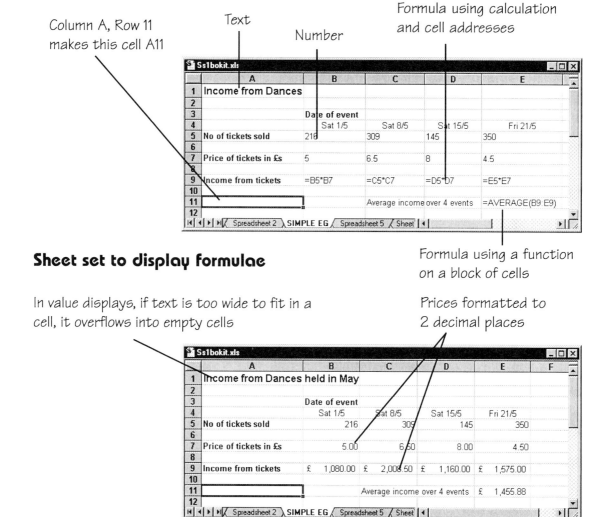

Column A, Row 11 makes this cell A11

Text

Number

Formula using calculation and cell addresses

Formula using a function on a block of cells

Sheet set to display formulae

In value displays, if text is too wide to fit in a cell, it overflows into empty cells

Prices formatted to 2 decimal places

Sheet as normally seen, displaying the results of the formulae

Calculating the Cost

The spreadsheet you will produce will be based on your own day trip and you should use the example below as guide to your design. The spreadsheet will be used to calculate initial costs. It will take into account:

Transport hire

The most complex part of the calculation, because:

➢ the number of people going on the trip will dictate the size of coach to hire

➢ for a given coach size there will be different costs per person as 31 in a 40 seater will cost more than 40 in a 40 seater.

This project assumes that there are three coach sizes: 20 seater, 35 seater and 60 seater.

Hire costs

Coach (20 seater)   £155

Coach (35 seater)   £190

Coach (60 seater)   £220

Numbers of students

At this stage of the trip you will not have a precise idea of numbers so base your calculations on multiples of 10, up to 60, i.e. 10, 20, 30, 40, 50, 60.

Underground fare and entrance fees

These are all on a per person basis.

Tube fare   £2.50 per person

Museum entrance   £4 per person (student)

From these figures you should be able to construct a spreadsheet.

Start by working out the calculations for one coach, then extend it to cover all three coach sizes and costs.

The spreadsheets that follow illustrate stages in spreadsheet production and design.

Spreadsheet 1: Layout and the type of formulae that you should use

➤ *These are not actual formulae*, they simply show what calculations have to be performed on what data.

➤ *Planning a sheet is essential.* In this case, the plan has been written into the spreadsheet. It could have equally well been drawn up on a sheet of paper.

➤ *There is no correct layout* so your design may vary from this. It will also contain your own figures.

Coach cost per person
= Coach cost / number of people

Working data – use your own
figures here

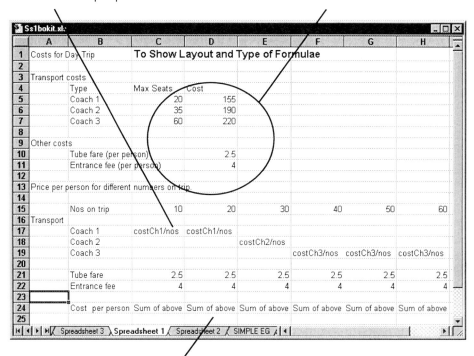

Total cost per person
Either add up the contents of the cells
= Coach cost + fare + fee
or use the SUM function to find the total of the cells above,
in rows 17 to 22

Spreadsheet 2: Actual formulae used to calculate the costs

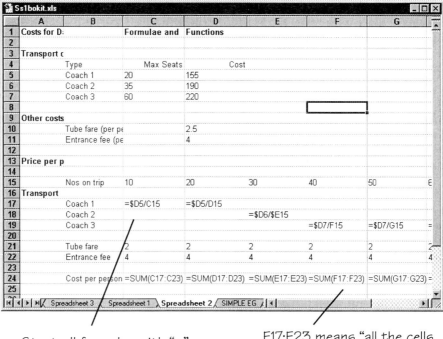

Start all formulae with "="

F17:F23 means "all the cells in Column F from 17 to 23"

Spreadsheet 3: "Raw" spreadsheet without any formatting

Spreadsheet 4: With formatting, borders and shades

right justified text

centre justified numbers

text made bold

font size changed

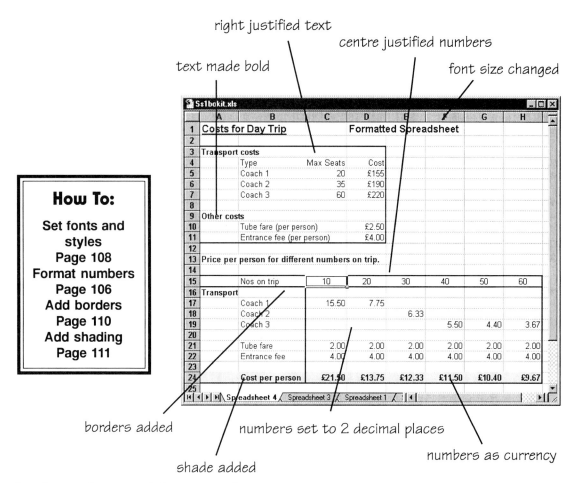

How To:

**Set fonts and styles
Page 108
Format numbers
Page 106
Add borders
Page 110
Add shading
Page 111**

borders added

numbers set to 2 decimal places

numbers as currency

shade added

Review of spreadsheet results

This spreadsheet clearly shows the difference in price caused by different numbers going. If only 10 went there would a high cost of over £20 per student, but if you double that number to 20 the price drops to under £14 per student, and if you get as many as 60 going you have a bargain price of under £10 per person! This illustrates the use of spreadsheets in terms of handling text, numbers and calculations. It provides an ideal tool to make "What if?" calculations.

Spreadsheet Tasks

Portfolio Builder

How To:

Copy cells
Page 112

How To:

Print
Page 118

Design a spreadsheet on the basis of that shown. Include your own figures and make modifications to suit your own trip.

When you are making the spreadsheet you must demonstrate that you can copy cells. A good example of cells that should be produced by copying is in the "Total costs per person" row. All the cells in this row will use the SUM function to add the column directly above. Type in the correct formula for the first "Total costs" cell (C24): @SUM(C17..C23) – *modified to your spreadsheet*. Now copy this cell across the whole row.

> **Level 3 only. When you look at the cells that you have just copied to, you will see that the spreadsheet has automatically altered the formulae so that the SUM always adds the figures in the column above. This is called "Relative cell addressing" and is important for Level 3. See below.**

Carry out the following spreadsheet tasks:

➤ Check for errors.

➤ Print out the spreadsheets in draft form, labelling them appropriately.

➤ Alter the layout and format to get maximum clarity.

➤ Save the spreadsheet with an appropriate name

Level 3 remember to include version number in filename.

➤ Print out the spreadsheets when fully formatted, and label appropriately.

➤ Change the spreadsheets options so that cell formulae are displayed. Print out and label.

Absolute and Relative Cell Addressing (Level 3)

Portfolio 2 Builder

When you copy your formulae and functions, spreadsheets, by default, assume that you require a relative copy and automatically alter cell references accordingly. Usually this is what is needed, but sometimes you do not want this relative referencing and must replace it with absolute cell addressing.

To explain this look at spreadsheet 5 and note row 19, which is shaded. If you were to copy the formulae in cell F19 "=D7/F15" across two columns, the spreadsheet would automatically change the cell address D7, as it moved across columns, to E7 and F7 respectively. In this case this is what you do not want, as D7 contains the cost of the coach and E7 and F7 are both empty. If we copy this cell normally we would get an error.

To tell that spreadsheet that you do not want the cells' addresses altered i.e. absolute addressing, use the "$" symbol. To stop D7 changing to E7 and then to F7, the D in the formulae should be prefixed by "$" and hence should read "=$D7/F15".

Spreadsheet 5

	A	B	C	D	E	F	G	H
1	Costs for Da		Absolute	& Relative	Cell Addressing			
2								
3	Transport c							
4		Type	Max Seats		Cost			
5		Coach 1	20	155				
6		Coach 2	35	190				
7		Coach 3	60	220				
8								
9	Other costs							
10		Tube fare (per p		2.5				
11		Entrance fee (p		4				
12								
13	Price per p							
14								
15		Nos on trip	10	20	30	40	50	60
16	Transport							
17		Coach 1	=$D5/C15	=$D5/D15				
18		Coach 2			=$D6/$E15			
19		Coach 3				=$D7/F15	=$D7/G15	=$D7/H15
20								
21		Tube fare	2	2	2	2	2	2
22		Entrance fee	2	2	2	2	2	2
23								
24		Cost per person	=SUM(C17:C23	=SUM(D17:D23	=SUM(E17:E23	=SUM(F17:F23	=SUM(G17:G23	=SUM(H17:H23
25								

Ss1bokit.xls

Spreadsheet 2 / SIMPLE EG \ Spreadsheet 5 / Sheet7 / Sheet8 / She

Note "$D7" only fixes addresses across columns (which in this example is all you need). If you want to fix row addresses as well you need "$" before the row number, i.e. "=D7/F15".

Retrieve your cost spreadsheet and edit it as follows:

➤ Remove the formulae in rows 17 and 19 (or your equivalents).

➤ Replace the relative cell formula in C17 with one that has absolute cell addressing i.e. "=$D5/C15".

➤ Copy this to the next cell, D17.

➤ Repeat for F19, using an absolute formula, "=$D7/F15".

➤ Copy this across the next two cells.

Check this is correct and save the spreadsheet file with a new appropriate name.

Make two printouts of the spreadsheet, one showing cells as displayed and the other showing formulae. Label the printouts.

Spreadsheet Templates (Level 3)

When you have collected all the reply slips from the students you should have an idea of the exact number of students who are going on your trip. This will enable you to calculate the exact cost per person. You can use your spreadsheet as a template and use this to calculate actual costs.

Let us imagine that 48 people are definitely committed to the trip. Retrieve your spreadsheet, and simply replace the "Nos on trip" figure of 50 with 48. This will then produce a cost per person figure exactly matching your numbers.

Embolden the whole column so that it stands out, save the file with a different and appropriate name. Print out the spreadsheet and label it.

Tracking Table: Spreadsheets

Ref. No. = Portfolio Builder Reference Number
El. No. = Element Number **PC** = Performance Criteria

Ref. No.	El. No.	PC	Range	Type of Evidence
📖 1	2.1	2	Information...numbers; Enter;	Printouts to show stages in spreadsheet design and production.
	3.1	2	Software...numbers;	
	2.2	1, 2, 3, 4	Information...numbers; Software...numbers; Edit;	Printouts to show stages in spreadsheet design and production.
	3.2	1, 2, 3, 4	Information...numbers; Software...numbers; Edit; Make calculations;	**Printouts of stages in spreadsheet design and production, including ones showing cell contents, i.e. formulae, functions. (Level 3)**
📖 2	3.2	3	Make calculations... ...absolute & relative cell addressing;	**Spreadsheet contents printout to show use of absolute and relative cell addressing. (Level 3)**
📖 3	3.1	5	Configure software;	**Printout of spreadsheet template. (Level 3)**

Databases

5

In this section you will use a database to keep records of all the people who have expressed an interest in going on the trip. A database is a powerful software tool that will process all the information rapidly and can provide you with lists of:

➢   who has paid their deposit

➢   who still owes the balance

➢   all those going, sorted on tutor groups

➢   addresses or classes of all students going, so that you can send update information (and bills).

Before you use a database there are two important stages that need to be gone through:

➢   designing and creating the database structure

➢   inputting the data.

Database Concepts

Databases cannot be fully understood unless you have a grasp of the basic concepts that underpin them. If you know about databases then skip this section, if not read on.

A database is simply a collection of data about a particular thing, for this example we will consider a database about a CD collection. A database file is made up of records, in this case each record would be about a particular CD, so if there were 25 CDs in the collection there would be 25 records. Each record has the same structure (see below):

CD Collection Database: Structure of Record

Heading or field name
Title
Artist
Year of release
Personal rating (1 to 5)

You can see that for this database each record is made up four "headings": title, artist, year and rating. These "headings" are actually called fields. The structure is decided upon when the database is first created. Every record will have this structure, but obviously the details that you fill in for each CD will be different.

The database also needs information on the type of data, and its size or length, that is going into each field. The full details of our record structure are then:

CD collection database: record structure

Field name	Type	Size
Title	Character	25
Artist	Character	35
Year of release	Numeric	4
Personal rating (1 to 5)	Numeric	1

 In Works, you do not have to set a length to text fields.

For the title and artist fields you have to make a sensible decision about their length. Some artists will have names over 25 characters long and some titles will be over 35 characters, but they will be in the minority and can be abbreviated.

When setting up a new database, start by looking carefully at a sample of your data. How should the information be broken down into fields?

Do you put a person's name into one field, or divide it into Surname and Forenames, or divide it into Title, Surname, First name and Second name?

How long does each field need to be? There is no point in making fields overlong – it wastes storage space and can make life difficult for setting up printouts. Check your sample. How big is the biggest item in each field? If necessary, can you abbreviate unusually long data? If you cannot, make each field half as long again as the longest items in the sample.

With numeric fields, are you storing integers (whole numbers), or ones with decimal fractions. If using decimals, how many decimal places do you need?

Each database package has its own set of data types, but generally they always include the following data types or attributes: character, numeric, date, logical. Sometimes the numeric data type is divided into different categories.

CD collection database: defined in Works

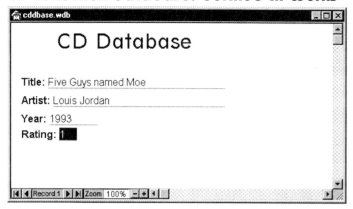

In Works you can limit the display width of text fields, and format the digits and decimals displays in number fields, but there are no actual limits to the length of data items.

✓		Title	Artist	Year	Rating
☑	1	Five Guys named Moe	Louis Jordan	1993	1
☑	2	Handful of Keys	Fats Waller	1992	2
☑	3	Django 1935-39	Django Reinhardt	1994	1
☑	4	Lets Sing Again	Fats Waller	1995	3
☑	5	I Need Your Lovin'	Conway Twitty	1993	5
☐	6				
☐	7				
☐	8				
☐	9				
☐	10				
☐	11				
☐	12				
☐	13				
☐	14				

Using a Database

All the data on your database will come from the completed reply slips from your last letter.

The design stage

This information will also dictate the structure of the database when you start to design it. Now you must decide WHAT information you want in your database.

To aid your design you should ask, "What do I want this database to do?"

The answer is, "To keep a record of all those going on the trip." In more detail this breaks down to:

➢   keeping a record of student payments

➢   being able to contact each student about the trip

➢   being able chase them up on their payments.

The details you will need for this will be:

> Last name
>
> First name
>
> Age
>
> Sex
>
> Address
>
> Course
>
> Tutor
>
> Paid £5 deposit?
>
> Date balance paid

A blank entry in this last field will denote they have not yet paid the balance.

It's your project and database and you may well have different details to those above (you may want to add telephone numbers), but they should roughly correspond. This will dictate a database structure as shown below, but remember, design your own to fit the needs of your trip.

Student database Version 1

Field Name	Field Type	Length
Last name	Character	15
First name	Character	15
Age	Numeric	2
Sex	Character	1
Address	Character	50
Course	Character	10
Tutor	Character	15
Paid £5 deposit?	Logical	(Yes or No)
Date balance paid	Date	

You will notice that some new field types are shown above.

Logical fields demand an entry of either Y(es) or N(o) or T(rue) or F(alse). "Have they paid their deposit?" requires a yes/no or true/false answer.

Date fields are automatically formatted into a date style, i.e. dd/mm/yy (e.g. 15/07/96). You can also test the values in the fields to see if they were before, after or on a given date.

Creating the Database and Inputting Data

Now the database work can start. You should be ready to;

➢ design your own database

➢ create it following the design above

➢ print out the database structure

➢ input data into it (from your reply slips)

➢ check data on input for accuracy

➢ save your database with appropriate name.

Manipulating and modifying the database

Now perform the following actions on the database, providing evidence for the skills used with labelled printouts.

1   Print out all students, all fields in the order that they are in the database.

2   Print out all students, showing the following fields: Surname, First name, Age and Course , in Course order.

3   Print out all students, Surname, Age, Course only in alphabetical order of Surname.

4   Print out all students, First name and Surname for all who have paid deposit.

5   Print out all students, First name, Surname and Tutor group for all who have NOT paid deposit.

6   Now add two students who have eventually decided to go on the trip.

7   Delete one student who cannot go after all.

8   One student has moved house in the last week, change his/her details accordingly.

9   Three additional students have paid their deposits.

10   Save these changes.

11   Print out whole database to show these changes.

12   Sort the database on tutor group order and print out those who have not paid their deposit.

There are illustrated examples on the next page.

44

Printout of the database after sample data has been first typed in. The records are still in the order in which they were entered.

Surname	First name	Age	Sex	Address	Course	Tutor	Deposit Paid	Date balance Pd
Jackson	Terry	17	M	26 Maybury Rd	GNVQ Adv Science	B Evans	Yes	12/08/96
Sharma	Rikki	28	M	13 Sunset Crescent	GNVQ Adv Science	B Evans	No	
Khan	Raxa	16	F	111 Firth St	BTEC Nat Dip IT	M White	Yes	
Morgan	Nicola	25	F	Flat 6, High st	BTEC Nat Dip IT	M White	Yes	11/28/96
Strong	Emma	16	F	52 Exeter St	GNVQ Adv Science	B Evans	No	
Plait	Karen	17	F	82 Whit Lane	BTEC Nat Dip CS	R Goodward	Yes	
Wood	Jan	16	F	89 Abse Rd	GNVQ Int Science	G Parvin	Yes	12/01/96
Bradley	Paul	17	M	16 Maybury Road	GNVQ Adv Sci	B Evans	No	
Regan	Paul	19	M	Flat 2a The polygon	GNVQ Adv Science	B Evans	Yes	12/01/96
Ali	Rino	16	M	The Trattoria, high	GNVQ Int Science	G Parvin	No	
Young	Neil	17	M	8 Cinnamon drive	GNVQ Adv Science	B Evans	Yes	
Everley	Kate	17	F	Flat 12, The Polygo	GNVQ Int Science	G Parvin	No	
Williamson	Robin	17	M	2 Duck Pond lane	GNVQ IntScience	G Parvin	Yes	12/10/96
Adams	Heather	18	F	25 Fairfields Rd	GNVQ Adv Science	B Evans	Yes	12/12/96
Walker	Sue	17	F	7 Sholing Drive	BTEC Nat Dip IT	M White	Yes	12/10/96
Pearce	Ben	17	M	67 Gunners Hill	BTEC Nat Dip CS	R Goodward	No	
Bush	Katherine	19	F	6 Hounds Crescent	GNVQ Adv Science	B Evans	No	

Surname	First name	Age	Course
Pearce	Ben	17	BTEC Nat Dip CS
Plait	Karen	17	BTEC Nat Dip CS
Khan	Raxa	16	BTEC Nat Dip IT
Morgan	Nicola	25	BTEC Nat Dip IT
Walker	Sue	17	BTEC Nat Dip IT
Bradley	Paul	17	GNVQ Adv Sci
Strong	Emma	16	GNVQ Adv Science
Regan	Paul	19	GNVQ Adv Science
Jackson	Terry	17	GNVQ Adv Science
Adams	Heather	18	GNVQ Adv Science
Sharma	Rikki	28	GNVQ Adv Science
Young	Neil	17	GNVQ Adv Science
Bush	Katherine	19	GNVQ Adv Science
Wood	Jan	16	GNVQ Int Science
Everley	Kate	17	GNVQ Int Science
Ali	Rino	16	GNVQ Int Science
Williamson	Robin	17	GNVQ IntScience

Printout of all records, showing Surname, First name, Age and Course. The records have been sorted into Course order.

How To

How To:

Design a report Page 132

Surname	Age	Course
Adams	18	GNVQ Adv Science
Ali	16	GNVQ Int Science
Bradley	17	GNVQ Adv Sci
Bush	19	GNVQ Adv Science
Everley	17	GNVQ Int Science
Jackson	17	GNVQ Adv Science
Khan	16	BTEC Nat Dip IT
Morgan	25	BTEC Nat Dip IT
Pearce	17	BTEC Nat Dip CS
Plait	17	BTEC Nat Dip CS
Regan	19	GNVQ Adv Science
Sharma	28	GNVQ Adv Science
Strong	16	GNVQ Adv Science
Walker	17	BTEC Nat Dip IT
Williamson	17	GNVQ IntScience
Wood	16	GNVQ Int Science
Young	17	GNVQ Adv Science

Printout of all records, showing Surname, Age and Course, sorted into Surname order.

How To:

Create filters Page 130

Surname	First name	Deposit Paid
Adams	Heather	Yes
Williamson	Robin	Yes
Young	Neil	Yes
Wood	Jan	Yes
Plait	Karen	Yes
Khan	Raxa	Yes
Walker	Sue	Yes
Regan	Paul	Yes
Morgan	Nicola	Yes
Jackson	Terry	Yes

Printout showing Surname, First name and Deposit paid, for those students who have paid.

Printout showing Surname, First name, Tutor and Deposit paid, for those students who have not yet paid their deposit.

Surname	First name	Tutor	Deposit Paid
Pearce	Ben	R Goodward	No
Strong	Emma	B Evans	No
Everley	Kate	G Parvin	No
Bradley	Paul	B Evans	No
Ali	Rino	G Parvin	No
Sharma	Rikki	B Evans	No
Bush	Katherine	B Evans	No

Printout of all records, showing all fields after the database has been updated. Sue Walker has gone.

How To:

Enter and edit data
Page 128

Two students have been added

One address has been changed

Surname	First name	Age	Sex	Address	Course	Tutor	Deposit Paid	Date balance Pd
Adams	Heather	18	F	25 Fairfields Rd	GNVQ Adv Science	B Evans	Yes	12/12/96
Ali	Rino	16	M	The Trattoria, high	GNVQ Int Science	G Parvin	No	
Bradley	Paul	17	M	16 Maybury Road	GNVQ Adv Sci	B Evans	Yes	
Bush	Katherine	19	F	6 Hounds Crescent	GNVQ Adv Science	B Evans	No	
Everley	Kate	17	F	71 Daisy Street	GNVQ Int Science	G Parvin	Yes	
Jackson	Terry	17	M	26 Maybury Rd	GNVQ Adv Science	B Evans	Yes	12/08/96
Khan	Raxa	16	F	111 Firth St	BTEC Nat Dip IT	M White	Yes	
Morgan	Nicola	25	F	Flat 6, High st	BTEC Nat Dip IT	M White	Yes	11/28/96
Painter	Jim	24	M	12 The Rise	NVQ IT	W Gavin	No	
Pearce	Ben	17	M	67 Gunners Hill	BTEC Nat Dip CS	R Goodward	No	
Plait	Karen	17	F	82 Whit Lane	BTEC Nat Dip CS	R Goodward	Yes	
Regan	Paul	19	M	Flat 2a The polygon	GNVQ Adv Science	B Evans	Yes	12/01/96
Sharma	Rikki	28	M	13 Sunset Crescent	GNVQ Adv Science	B Evans	No	
Smith	Pat	22	F	55 Exeter St	NVQ IT	W Gavin	Yes	03/05/97
Strong	Emma	16	F	52 Exeter St	GNVQ Adv Science	B Evans	Yes	
Williamson	Robin	17	M	2 Duck Pond lane	GNVQ IntScience	G Parvin	Yes	12/10/96
Wood	Jan	16	F	89 Abse Rd	GNVQ Int Science	G Parvin	Yes	12/01/96
Young	Neil	17	M	8 Cinnamon drive	GNVQ Adv Science	B Evans	Yes	

Three more have paid their deposits

Printout of those students who have not yet paid their deposit, sorted into Tutor group order. All fields are shown except Date balance paid.

Surname	First name	Age	Sex	Address	Course	Tutor	Deposit Paid
Strong	Emma	16	F	52 Exeter St	GNVQ Adv Science	B Evans	No
Ali	Rino	16	M	The Trattoria, high	GNVQ Int Science	G Parvin	No
Pearce	Ben	17	M	67 Gunners Hill	BTEC Nat Dip CS	R Goodward	No
Sharma	Rikki	28	M	13 Sunset Crescent	GNVQ Adv Science	B Evans	No
Painter	Jim	24	M	12 The Rise	NVQ IT	W Gavin	No

Tracking Table: Databases

Ref. No. = Portfolio Builder Reference Number
El. No. = Element Number **PC** = Performance Criteria

Ref. No.	El. No.	PC	Range	Type of Evidence
📖 1	2.1	4	Software;	Database designed. **For level 2 this design can be given**.
	3.1	4, 5	Configure software;	
📖 2	2.1	2, 4	Information; Enter; Software;	Creation of database, data input and whole database printed out.
	3.1	2, 4	Information; Enter; Software;	
📖 3	2.2	4	Find; Edit: Reorganise	Editing, manipulation, searching, sorting and retrieving data from database, as shown by the seven printouts asked for.
	3.2	4	Find; Edit: Reorganise	
	2.3	1, 2, 3	Information; Requirements; Software;	
	3.3	2, 3, 4	Information; Requirements; Software;	

Word Processing and Spreadsheets Combined

6

This section takes your word processing and spreadsheet skills a stage further, and it also looks at combining the output from different packages into one document. In this case it means importing a spreadsheet and its accompanying graph into a word processed report.

Scenario

On the basis of the success of your day trip you have been encouraged to look at the possibility of organising a much larger, more ambitious trip, a visit to a European city. Before you take this idea any further you have been asked to carry out two investigations:

➤ a poll of students to discover which European city they would most like to visit

➤ a report on a possible visit to Paris indicating: costs, different ways of getting there, what to see when in Paris.

Which European city?

The aim of this undertaking is to:

➤ design a questionnaire to find which city students want to visit

➤ collect and collate the data from this questionnaire

➤ use a spreadsheet to analyse the results

➤ display the results graphically

➤ write a short report on the results, importing the spreadsheet and graph into the report.

Questionnaire Design

The questionnaire will ask students which city they would most want to visit. Give them a choice of four or five cities. Make your own decisions but a possible selection might be: London, Paris, Brussels, Amsterdam. You will analyse the results into categories based on the student's main subject. So the questionnaire must ask for choice of city, student's main subject and student's name. A typical questionnaire might look like this, but design your own.

European Visit
Destination Questionnaire

Year Two GNVQ groups are planning a two-day visit to a major European city. We want your opinion on which city you would most like to visit.

Please complete the questionnaire below and return it to either Joy Pearce or Danny Parsons.

Thanks.

Name: ....

Course Studied: ....

Please tick one only

London   ☐
Paris   ☐
Brussels   ☐
Amsterdam   ☐

Return to Joy or Danny as soon as possible.
Thanks again.
GNVQ Yr 2

You will need to get around 50 replies to produce a good statistical analysis. When you have collected the completed forms you will need to collate the results in a table similar to that below, but once again modify it to suit your own ideas.

Sample results have been included in this table:

Subject Group	London	Paris	Amsterdam	Brussels
GNVQ lev. 2	11	22	10	2
GNVQ lev. 3	4	34	25	12
NVQ & others	23	28	32	25
Total				

The total line has been deliberately left blank.

Calculate and Graph

Portfolio **2** Builder

How To:
**Create graphs
Page 122**

Enter these results into a spreadsheet.

You will now use the spreadsheet's facilities to:

➢ Calculate the totals

➢ Draw two graphs:

Graph 1 A pie chart which shows the numbers voted for each city.

Graph 2 A bar chart showing the breakdown of the votes on a group basis.

Your graphs should have:

➢ Titles

➢ Legends

➢ Appropriate axes

➢ Appropriate shading.

Save your spreadsheets and graphs.

See examples below.

Chart 1: Votes for each city

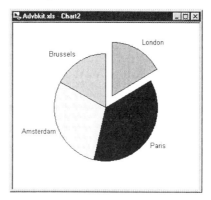

Use the Totals line
as the data for
the Pie Chart.

Chart 2: Breakdown of votes

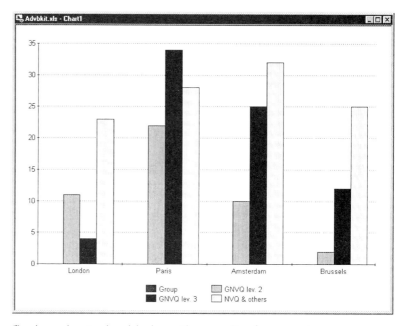

How To:

Create graphs
Page 122

The bar chart should show the results from each group.

Report on planned European visit

Write a brief report about this survey. Say how it was done, when it was done and the groups targeted. There should then be a section discussing the results and referring to the spreadsheet results. Import the spreadsheet and the two graphs into the report. You will need to position and size these carefully so they look part of a professionally produced report.

Level 3 Only: Paris Visit

Portfolio Builder 4

The aim of this section is:

collect information by accessing a remote database.

Write a multi-page report that has *headers and footers*, which include page numbers and date as well as a report title.

Headers and footers are formatted text that a word processor automatically puts at the head and foot of every page. You define what is in these and the position (left, centre or right) of the different parts. You can have headers without footers and footers without headers.

Collecting Information on the Paris trip

To get to Paris you have to cross the Channel and there are several ways of doing this: ferry, hovercraft, Sea Cat, plane, Channel Tunnel. Find the price for a return trip for each of these. Use a spreadsheet's graphing facility to illustrate the relative prices in a graphical form. Later you will incorporate this graph into your report.

Now you need to collect information about places of interest you could visit when in Paris. This is an ideal opportunity to get information from a remote database. If your college has Internet access then you will find plenty of information about Paris, its sights, museums and galleries. Collect what you think is relevant and useful to incorporate into your report.

Now you are ready to produce your Paris report. Aim to make it at least three pages long, the imported graph will help, but you can import clip art graphics as well. The report should have the following sections:

➢ How to get there; the cheapest route

➢ What to do when there

➢ Passport issues (you will need to find out about these)

➢ Allowances for food and drink on the trip.

If you have time you may want to investigate where you would stay and the prices of cheap hotels.

Tracking Table: Word Processing and Spreadsheets

Ref. No. = Portfolio Builder Reference Number
El. No. = Element Number **PC** = Performance Criteria

Ref. No.	El. No.	PC	Range	Type of Evidence
📖 1	2.3	1	Information; Requirements;	Print out of questionnaire showing layout and design.
	3.3	1, 2	Information; Requirements; Prepare... ...documents;	
📖 2	2.2	1, 3	Find; Information;	Printout of spreadsheets and spreadsheet plus accompanying graphs.
	3.2	1, 3	Find; Information; Make calcs;	
	2.3	1, 2, 3	All	
	3.3	1, 2, 3, 4	All	
📖 3	2.2	6	Combine... ...different.;	Report document which contains combined/merged files from different packages (word processor and spreadsheet).
	3.2	6	Combine... ...different.;	
📖 4	3.2	1	Find... ...remote database;	Information obtained from a remote database. **(Level 3)**
	3.3	1	Prepare...paginating and date stamping	A multi-page report with headers and footers as described. **(Level 3)**

Evaluate the Use of IT

7

The final section of your IT Key Skills project is an "Evaluation of Information Technology". This is best done by looking at the IT you used throughout this project. For Level 3 this has to be extended by looking at three other examples in more detail.

Use of IT in this Project

Write a report on the use of IT throughout this project. The report should cover the following areas:

➢ Why you used IT in the project.

➢ Describe the packages you used and explain how they helped in your project. Describe some of the useful facilities of these packages, and give two examples of how this helped you in your overall task, e.g. spell checking in word processing and summing functions in spreadsheets.

➢ Contrast your use of packages in this project with having to do the whole activity manually, i.e. without computers.

➢ Explain any problems you encountered when using IT. Examples of problems are errors, faults in equipment and loss of information. Your error log should come in very handy here, see **General IT skills** section.

➢ Compare IT and non-IT processes in terms of speed, accuracy, ease of use and effort, include in this account a brief description of how IT is used in industry and commerce. An excellent source of comparisons is the working office, where typewriters have been taken over by word processors, filing cabinets by disk drives, conventional post and courier by E-mail and fax.

➢ Explain the importance of working safely in line with good working practices. Also describe safety in terms of the people using the equipment, the safety of the equipment itself and of the information kept on computers.

Level 3 Only: Extended Evaluation

Include in your report on IT in the project a justification for the use of IT.

Report on IT in industry/commerce

Write a report evaluating three examples of information management/processing comparing the manual (non-IT) and IT method.

There are many possible examples to choose from. Some possible ones where there is great scope to compare manual systems with computerised ones are: the office, the banking system, modern supermarkets where bar coding has revolutionised the checkout process as well as stock control.

In the report also examine the impact of IT in terms of effectiveness, costs, and effects on employment. Consider the benefits and the disadvantages to individuals and organisations.

Tracking Table: Evaluate the Use of IT

Ref. No. = Portfolio Builder Reference Number
El. No. = Element Number **PC** = Performance Criteria

Ref. No.	El. No.	PC	Range	Type of Evidence
📖 1	2.4	1, 2, 3, 4, 5	All	Report on use of IT within this project. Details as outlined in text.
	3.4	1, 2, 4, 5, 6	All	
📖 2	3.4	1, 3.	Compare; Methods; Evaluate; Systems.	Report on the use of IT in business and commerce. Considering IT and non-IT methods and effect on individuals. Details as outlined in text. **(Level 3)**

Files and directories

8

The techniques used to manage files and directories are almost identical in Windows 3.1 and Windows 95. In this section, the text applies to both systems, but there are separate illustrations for each.

How to manage files

If you want to see what is on your disks, reorganise your storage, move, copy or delete files, use File Manager (Windows 3.1) or Explorer (Windows 95). Both do the same range of jobs, though in slightly different ways.

Windows 3.1 File Manager

File Manager lets you open windows for each of your drives – you can even have several windows displaying different views of the same drive. This multiple display can be useful when copying or moving files between directories or drives. You can open a new window at any time, by double-clicking on a drive icon.

You may only have A: (the floppy drive) and C: (the main hard drive) in your system.

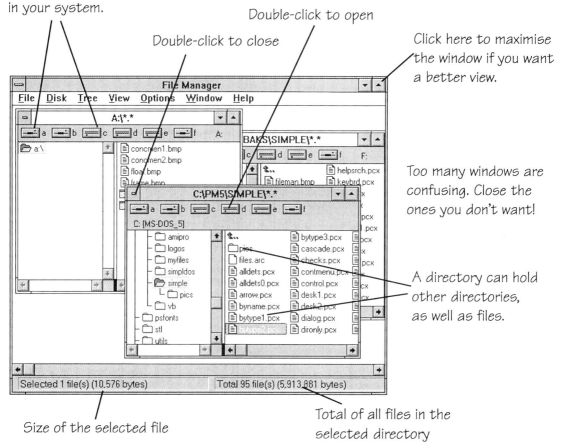

Double-click to open

Double-click to close

Click here to maximise the window if you want a better view.

Too many windows are confusing. Close the ones you don't want!

A directory can hold other directories, as well as files.

Size of the selected file

Total of all files in the selected directory

The Tree pane

Each window has two panes. On the left is the *Tree*, showing the directory structure. The drive letter (normally C:\) is the *root* – at the top! Branching off from this are directories for each application or major group of files. Some of these directories will have sub-directories branching off from them.

You can expand branches to show the sub-directories, or collapse them so that only the top-level directory is visible.

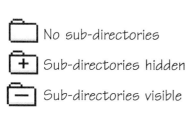

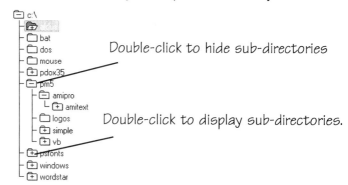

Double-click to hide sub-directories

Double-click to display sub-directories.

The Directory pane

View > Names only means open the **View** menu and click on **Names only**

On the right is the Directory pane, showing the contents of the selected directory.

Use **View > Names only** to display more files at once.

Use **View > All File Details** to see the size and date of files.

Point here to get the split pointer...

... then drag to resize

The window is normally split evenly between the two panes, but you can move the dividing line to change the balance. If you want to see more file information, a bigger Directory pane helps; if you are concentrating on the structure, a bigger Tree pane is useful.

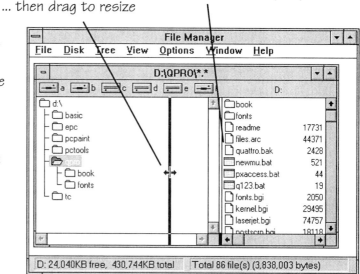

Windows 95 – Explorer

Windows 95 Folders =
Windows 3.1 Directories

This is closely related to File Manager of Windows 3.1. It gives a dual display, with the folder structure on the left and the contents of the current folder on the right. Explorer only displays the contents of one folder, but you can run two or more copies of it at once. This is useful when moving or copying files from one part of the system to another.

Explorer can access the folders in all of the drives attached to your computer, and to any that may be accessible to you over a network.

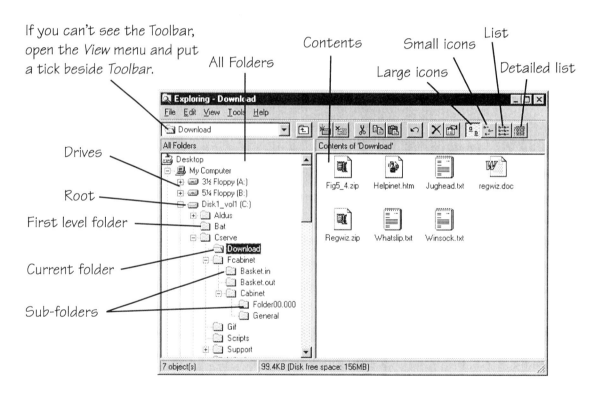

If you can't see the Toolbar, open the View menu and put a tick beside Toolbar.

All Folders

Contents

Small icons

Large icons

List

Detailed list

Drives

Root

First level folder

Current folder

Sub-folders

The Contents pane

The right-hand pane shows the contents of the currently selected folder. You can change the display using options on the **View** menu, or the Toolbar buttons.

➢ Use **Large icons** for ease of recognition

➢ either **Small icons** or the **List** to see lots of files

➢ the **Detailed list** to see the size or date of files.

The All Folders pane

The left-hand pane shows the structure of drives and folders. The drive letter (normally C:\) is the *root* – at the top! Below and right are folders for each application or major group of files. Some of these will have sub-folders branching off from them.

Click ⊞ by a folder to open its set of sub-folders.

Click ⊟ by an expanded folder to collapse it down.

Collapse whole set

Collapse folder

Expand sub-folder

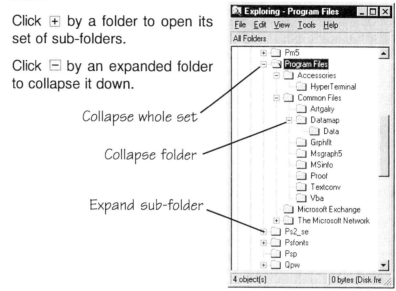

My Computer

This is the same as the Contents pane of Explorer. Moving around the system is limited. You can open any sub-folders displayed in the pane, and move back up through the level, using the drop-down list.

My Computer is useful if you just want to do some work in one folder, but for most purposes, Explorer is the better tool.

Switch to other drives or folders higher up the same path.

This is the Detailed List display – the other views can also be used.

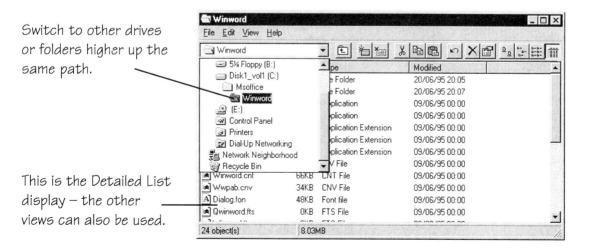

How to create directories

Modern hard disks can store thousands of files – even floppy disks can hold dozens. This storage must be organised if you want to be able to find files easily. The solution is to create a directory (or folder, Windows 95 calls them), for each major application or group of files.

If you do not have a directory specially for your GNVQ files, you should create one now.

First decide where the new directory will go. Should it be at the top level, coming straight off the root? Should it be a sub-directory of an existing directory?

Windows 3.1

Directories are created in File Manager.

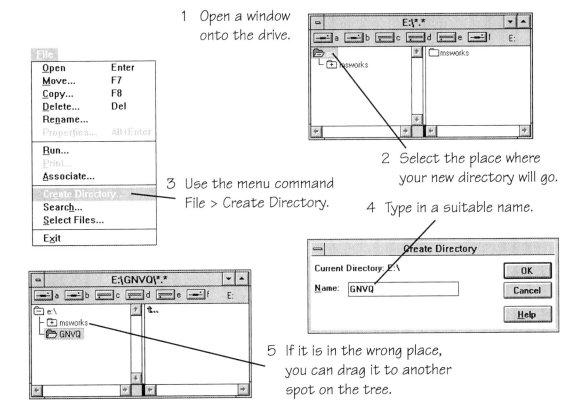

1 Open a window onto the drive.

2 Select the place where your new directory will go.

3 Use the menu command File > Create Directory.

4 Type in a suitable name.

5 If it is in the wrong place, you can drag it to another spot on the tree.

Windows 95

You can create your new folder in either Explorer or My Computer. The process is exactly the same.

When first created, a folder is always called "New Folder". This is not a lot of use, but it is easy to change the name.

2 From the File menu, select New then Folder.

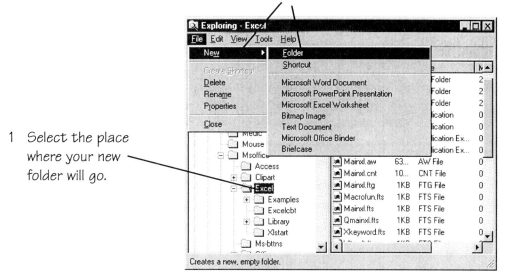

1 Select the place where your new folder will go.

3 Use the menu command File > Rename.

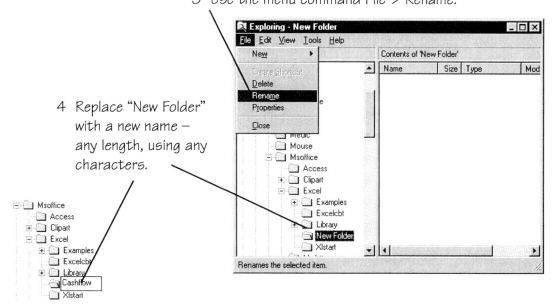

4 Replace "New Folder" with a new name – any length, using any characters.

How to save files

While you are working on a document, its data is stored in the computer's memory. When you exit from Works, the memory is wiped. You should keep a copy of every document that you produce when working on your GNVQ. To do this, you must save it to disk.

The process is almost always the same, for all Windows applications and all types of document.

Windows 3.1

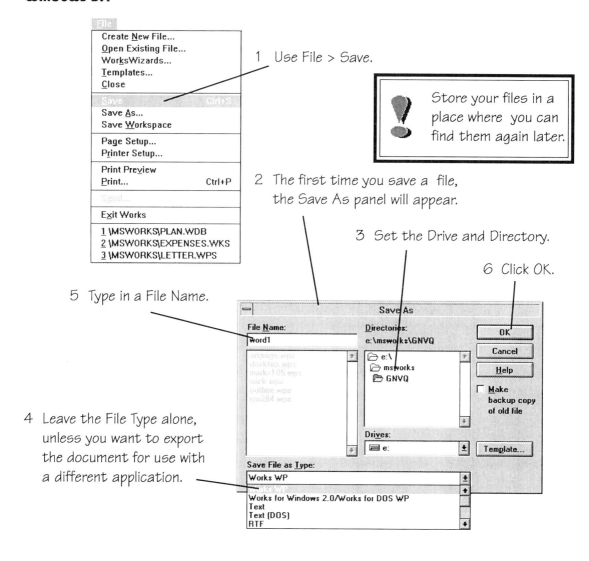

1 Use File > Save.

Store your files in a place where you can find them again later.

2 The first time you save a file, the Save As panel will appear.

3 Set the Drive and Directory.

6 Click OK.

5 Type in a File Name.

4 Leave the File Type alone, unless you want to export the document for use with a different application.

Windows 95

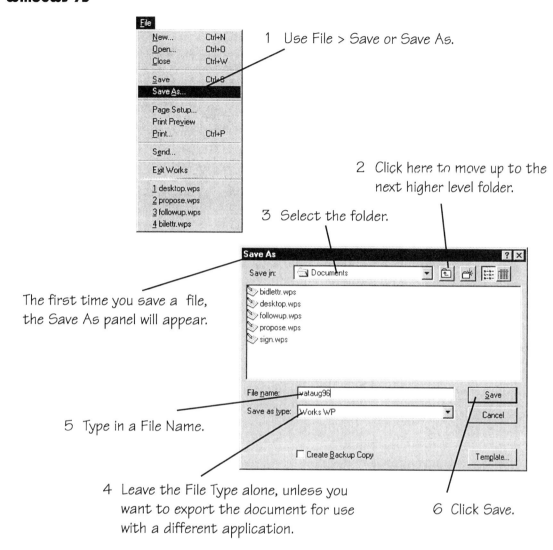

1 Use File > Save or Save As.

2 Click here to move up to the next higher level folder.

3 Select the folder.

The first time you save a file, the Save As panel will appear.

5 Type in a File Name.

4 Leave the File Type alone, unless you want to export the document for use with a different application.

6 Click Save.

Save and Save As

To re-save an existing file, just click the 🖫 button. The new file replaces the earlier copy.

If you have edited a document and want to keep a copy of the original, as well as the new version, use **File > Save As** and give it a different name.

How to open files

To get your documents back for editing, you must open their files. You can do this from the startup panel (Task Launcher in Windows 95), or using the File menu, during a working session.

Windows 3.1

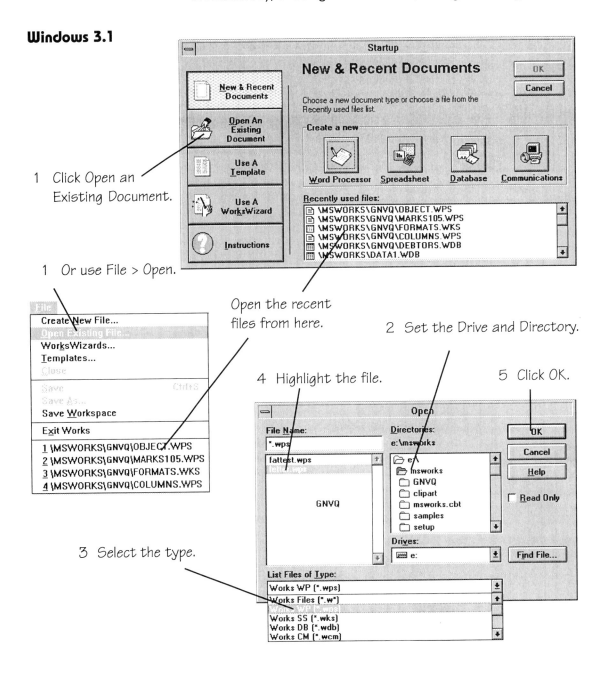

1 Click Open an Existing Document.

1 Or use File > Open.

Open the recent files from here.

2 Set the Drive and Directory.

4 Highlight the file.

5 Click OK.

3 Select the type.

Windows 95

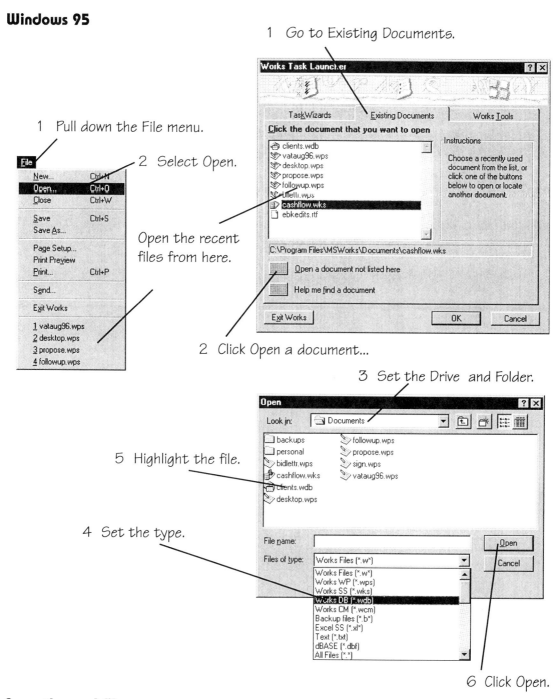

1 Go to Existing Documents.

1 Pull down the File menu.

2 Select Open.

Open the recent files from here.

2 Click Open a document...

3 Set the Drive and Folder.

5 Highlight the file.

4 Set the type.

6 Click Open.

Recently used files

In both versions, there are lists of the most recently used files on the File menu and in the startup panel. To open one of these, just click on it.

How to copy and back up

Selecting sets of files

Before you can copy (or move or delete) a file, you must select it by clicking on it. If you want to copy several files at once, you can select them as a group. This comes in useful when you want to back up a day's work by copying the new files to a floppy disk, or move a group from one directory to another, or delete a load of files that are not wanted.

There are two simple ways to select a group.

➢ Use the **[Shift]** key to select a block of adjacent files

➢ Use the **[Ctrl]** key to select a scattered set.

Both methods work in all versions of Windows.

[Shift] selecting

1 Click on the file at the top left.

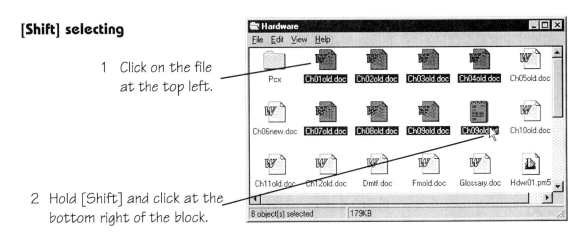

2 Hold [Shift] and click at the bottom right of the block.

[Ctrl] selecting

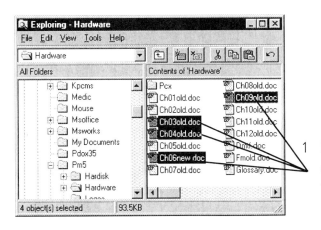

1 Hold [Ctrl] and click on each file that you want.

Copying files

You can copy a file from one disk to another by simply dragging it across the File Manger/Explorer window.

If you drag a file to a new directory on the same disk, you must hold [Ctrl] while you drag to copy it. If the [Ctrl] key is not held down, the file will be moved.

Windows 3.1 File Manager

1 Open windows for the source and target disks.

4 Select the file.

3 Open the source directory.

2 Adjust the target window so you can see the directory you want to copy into.

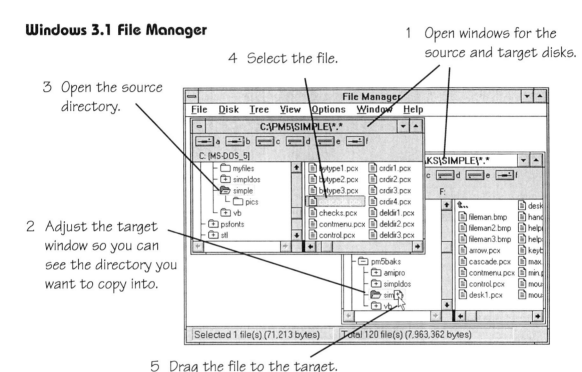

5 Drag the file to the target.

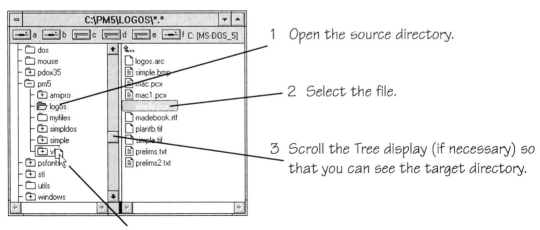

1 Open the source directory.

2 Select the file.

3 Scroll the Tree display (if necessary) so that you can see the target directory.

4 Hold [Ctrl] and drag the file to the target.

Windows 95 Explorer

1 Open the source folder and select the file(s) to be copied.

2 Scroll the All Folders display so that you can see the target disk or folder.

3 If you are copying within the same disk, hold [Ctrl].

4 Drag the file to the target.

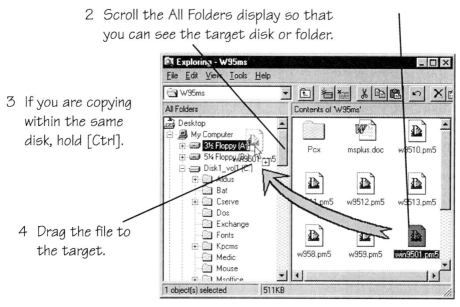

You can "Send" files to a floppy!

1 Select the files.

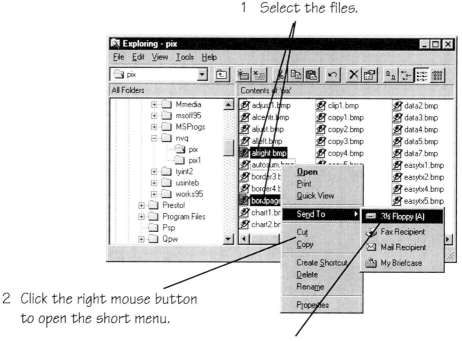

2 Click the right mouse button to open the short menu.

3 Point to Send to and select Floppy Disk.

How to start a new document

New documents begin at the Startup panel (Task Launcher in Windows 95). This will open automatically when you first run Works. If Works is already active, use the File > New menu command to open the panel.

For standard business documents, it is sometimes easiest to use a Wizard. This will do the layout and formatting for you – and may even give you some sample contents.

Windows 3.1

Click a button to open an application and start a new document.

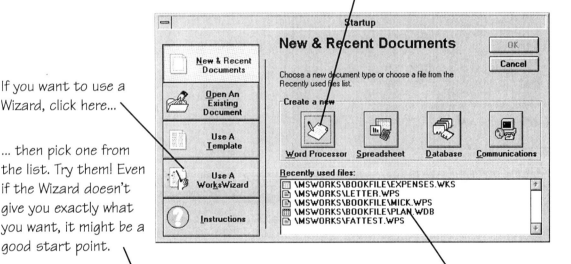

If you want to use a Wizard, click here...

... then pick one from the list. Try them! Even if the Wizard doesn't give you exactly what you want, it might be a good start point.

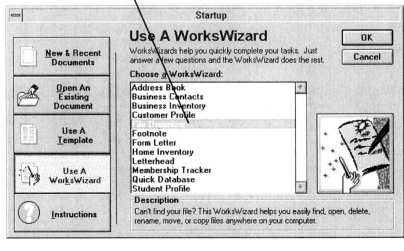

The last few files that you used can be opened from here.

Windows 95

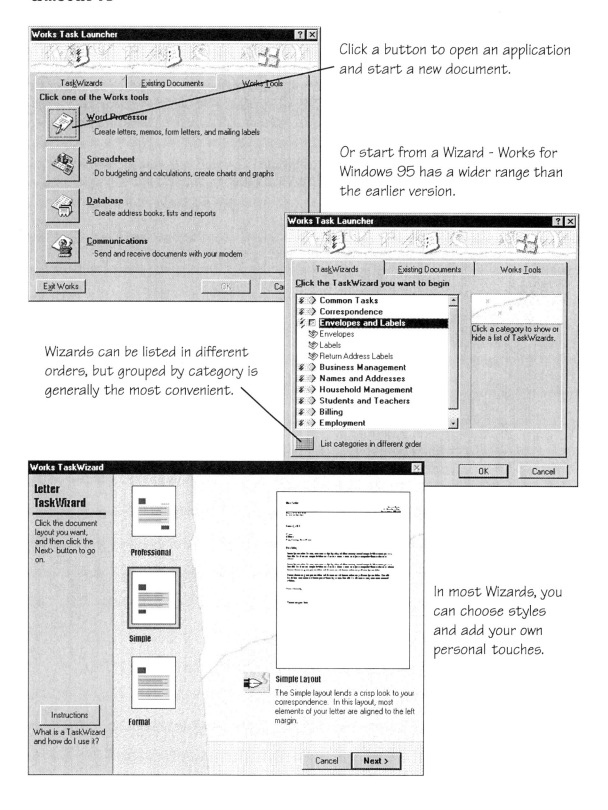

Click a button to open an application and start a new document.

Or start from a Wizard - Works for Windows 95 has a wider range than the earlier version.

Wizards can be listed in different orders, but grouped by category is generally the most convenient.

In most Wizards, you can choose styles and add your own personal touches.

The Help pages

9

Windows 3.1

Windows 95

How to use Help Contents

Help is one thing you will never be short of in Works.

Using the Contents is the best approach when you are trying to find out how to do something, but aren't sure of the terminology. It starts with a list of the major areas of help on the application you have open at the time. From here you can work through to the Help page about a specific topic.

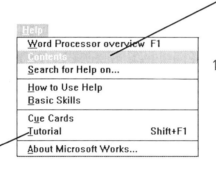

1 Open the Help menu and select Contents.

The Tutorial covers many of the basic skills and concepts and is well worth spending a little while on when you first start.

2 At the Contents list, click on Basic Skills, or the name of the application for which you need help.

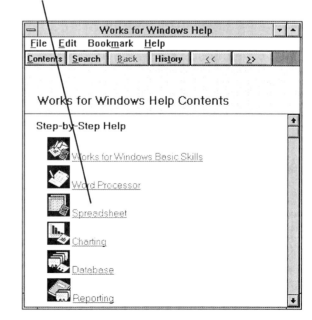

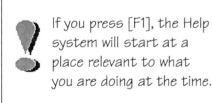
If you press [F1], the Help system will start at a place relevant to what you are doing at the time.

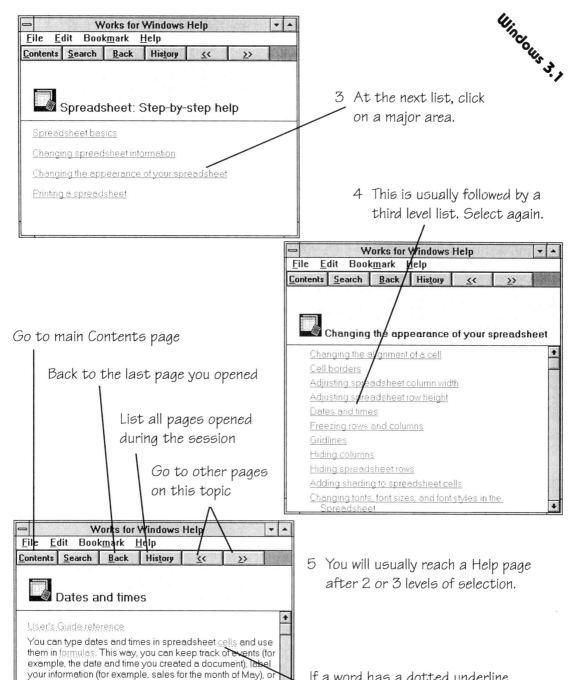

3 At the next list, click on a major area.

4 This is usually followed by a third level list. Select again.

Go to main Contents page

Back to the last page you opened

List all pages opened during the session

Go to other pages on this topic

5 You will usually reach a Help page after 2 or 3 levels of selection.

If a word has a dotted underline, clicking on it shows its Glossary entry. Anything with a solid underline will take you to another Help page.

How to search for Help

The Search route can be a quicker way to get to the right information, as long as you know what you are looking for. You don't have to be that exact, as the Help pages are cross-referenced. You can often get to the same page from several different start points, and once into the pages, you can easily switch between related topics.

To start searching, open the *Help* menu and select *Search*, or click on the *Search* button on any Help page.

1 Start to type a word that describes the topic you are interested in.

2 Highlight a topic and click the Show Topics button. The related pages will be listed in the Go To pane.

As you type, the list of topics will adjust to show those that start with the same letters.

Search

Type a **w**ord, or select one from the list. Then choose Show Topics.

fi

fields: moving
fields: naming
file (document): opening
file format
file: closing
file: creating

Close

Show Topics

Select a **t**opic, then choose Go To.

Go To

Save As command (File menu)
Save Command (File menu)

If necessary, scroll through the list until you find a likely topic.

3 Highlight a topic in the new list and click Go To to open the Help page.

If you can't see anything promising, try a different key word for the topic.

How to use Cue Cards

Cue Cards can be very useful when you are tackling a new job for the first time, as they will take you one step at a time through the process – rather as this book does. The catch to them is that they take up a fair chunk of screen space. There is not much you can do about this, as the cards are of fixed size, though you can shrink them down to icons if you want them out of the way for a moment.

1 Open the Help menu and select Cue Cards.

2 The first card will introduce the concept and ask if you want to use the cards. Accept the offer, for now.

3 Menu cards carry ☐ buttons. Click on these to select a task. Steps cards will often carry a ☐ **Next >** ☐ button. Click here when you have completed the steps.

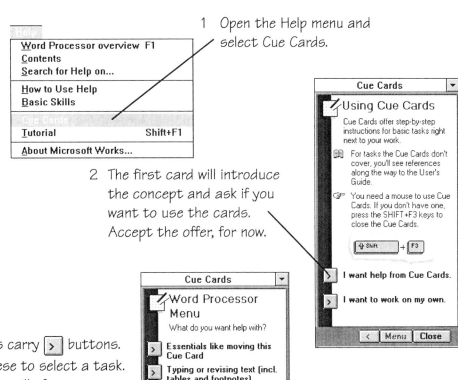

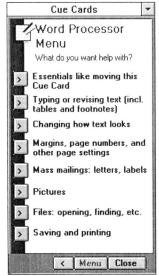

How to use the Help panel

In Works for Windows 95, Help is always at hand. The Help panel is normally open all the time, for instant access. If you need the space more than the help, it can be shrunk out of the way, or completely hidden. In either case, it can be reopened easily at any point.

Take a few minutes to view the Introduction to Works.
It gives a good overview of the system.

The Forum is an on-line service. You must have an Internet connection to use this.

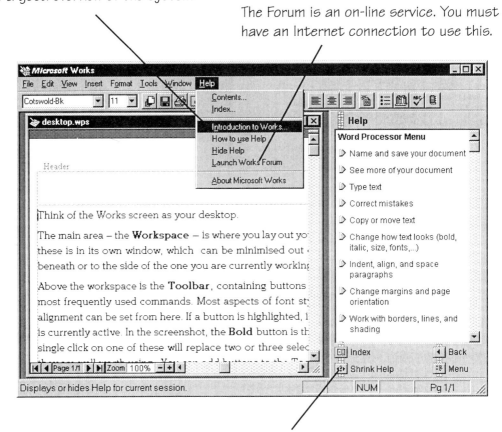

Click to shrink the Help panel out of the way.
Click again to open up a shrunken panel.

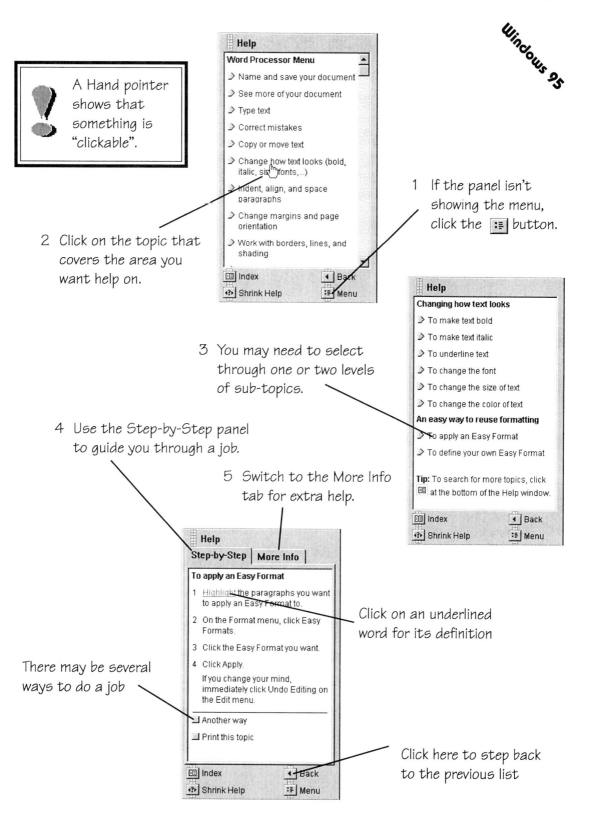

77

Windows 95

Files and directories

The Help Pages

Word Processor

Spreadsheet

Database

A Hand pointer shows that something is "clickable".

Help

Word Processor Menu

> Name and save your document
> See more of your document
> Type text
> Correct mistakes
> Copy or move text
> Change how text looks (bold, italic, size, fonts,...)
> Indent, align, and space paragraphs
> Change margins and page orientation
> Work with borders, lines, and shading

📖 Index   ◀ Back
❮❯ Shrink Help   ⠿ Menu

2 Click on the topic that covers the area you want help on.

1 If the panel isn't showing the menu, click the ⠿ button.

Help

Changing how text looks

> To make text bold
> To make text italic
> To underline text
> To change the font
> To change the size of text
> To change the color of text

An easy way to reuse formatting

> To apply an Easy Format
> To define your own Easy Format

Tip: To search for more topics, click 📖 at the bottom of the Help window.

📖 Index   ◀ Back
❮❯ Shrink Help   ⠿ Menu

3 You may need to select through one or two levels of sub-topics.

4 Use the Step-by-Step panel to guide you through a job.

5 Switch to the More Info tab for extra help.

Help

| Step-by-Step | More Info |

To apply an Easy Format

1 Highlight the paragraphs you want to apply an Easy Format to.

2 On the Format menu, click Easy Formats.

3 Click the Easy Format you want.

4 Click Apply.

If you change your mind, immediately click Undo Editing on the Edit menu.

▬ Another way
▬ Print this topic

📖 Index   ◀ Back
❮❯ Shrink Help   ⠿ Menu

Click on an underlined word for its definition

There may be several ways to do a job

Click here to step back to the previous list

How to search the Index

You can just scroll through the Index, but it's quicker to focus it by typing in a word to describe what you are looking for. You don't have to be that exact, as you can often get to the same page from different start points, and once into the pages, you can switch between related topics.

2 Start to type a word that describes the topic. The list of topics will show those that start with the same letters.

4 If necessary, open a folder to see its set of topics.

3 Scroll through the list until you can see a likely topic.

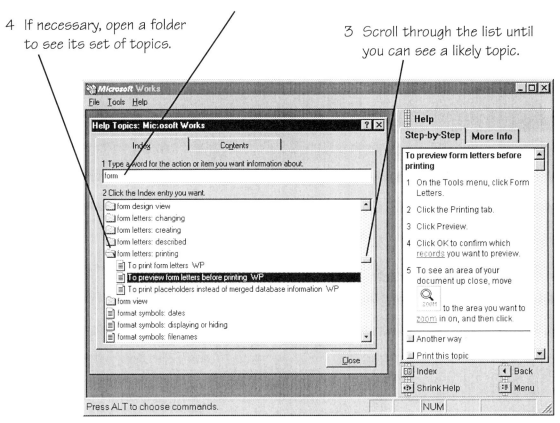

5 Select a topic to display it in the Help panel.

1 Open the Help menu and select Index, or click on the [📖] Index button on the Help panel.

How to use Help Contents

In the **Contents**, the Help pages have been organised into a hierarchy of topics. Start by selecting the tool, then work your way down through the levels of folders to focus on the help you need.

1 Open the Help menu and select Contents,

or

If you have been using the Index, switch to the Contents tab.

3 Click on the folders to open (or reclose) them, until you find the topic you want.

4 Click on a topic to display it in the Help panel.

2 Click on a tool in the list or on its button to open its folders.

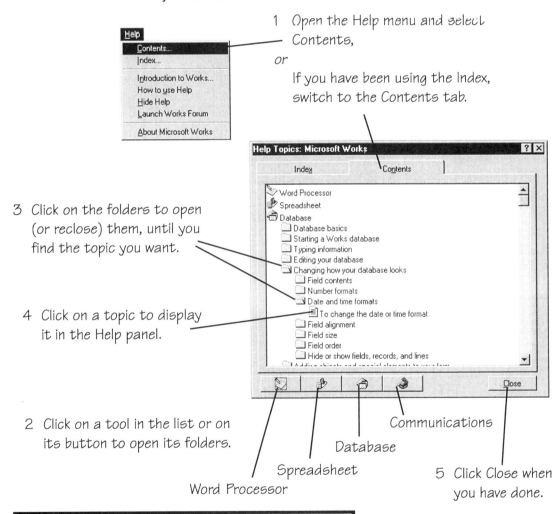

Communications

Database

Spreadsheet

Word Processor

5 Click Close when you have done.

 Contents gives you access to help on all the major tools, unlike the Help page Menu which only covers the current tool.

How to get other Help

When working in a dialog box, you can get help on any options within the box.

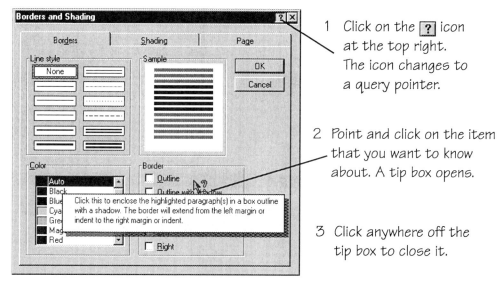

1 Click on the ? icon
   at the top right.
   The icon changes to
   a query pointer.

2 Point and click on the item
   that you want to know
   about. A tip box opens.

3 Click anywhere off the
   tip box to close it.

The Help systems for ClipArt, WordArt and the other minor tools also have a Find tab. This searches for keywords in help pages.

1 Start to type a word.

2 Select a matching word.

3 Double-click to display a
   Help page from this list.

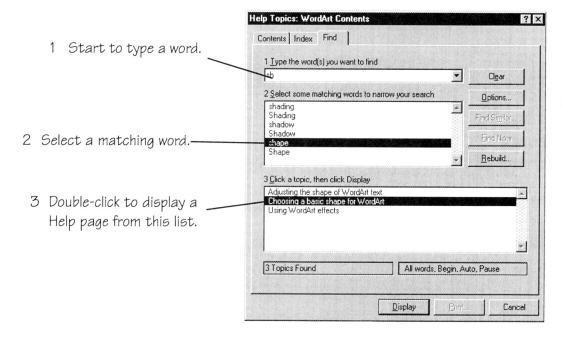

Works Word Processor

10

 From here on, almost all of the illustrations are taken from Works for Windows 95. If you are using Works for Windows 3.1, the screens will appear slightly different, but the same features will be present.

How to enter and edit text

When you start a new document, there will be nothing in the working area, except the outlines of the text and header areas.

The settings shown here apply to any text you type now. You can change them at any time, and you can select words and paragraphs later and change their settings.

Font name   Font size   Alignment   Ruler, showing tab, indents and margins

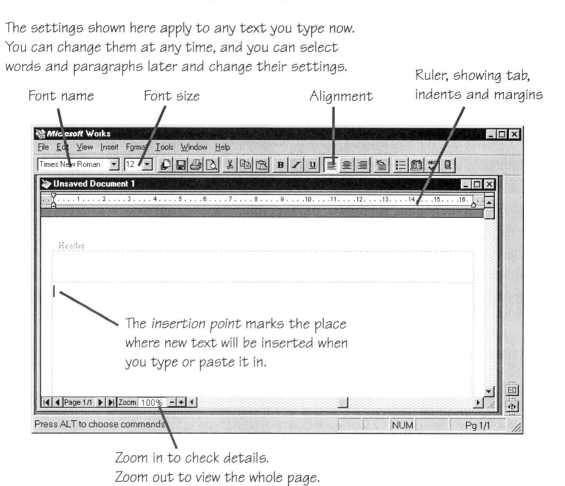

The insertion point marks the place where new text will be inserted when you type or paste it in.

Zoom in to check details.
Zoom out to view the whole page.

Entering text

Don't think of the screen as a blank sheet of paper. You cannot start typing anywhere you like. The insertion point can only move where there is text or spaces. If you want to start over on the right, type spaces or tabs to push the insertion point across. If you want to start lower down on, press **[Enter]** to move it down.

Wordwrap

When you reach the end of the line, just keep typing. The system will wrap the text round onto the next line for you. Do not press **[Enter]** until you reach the end of a paragraph.

The advantage of wordwrap is that if you later decide to change the width between the margins, the text will be relaid so that it still flows smoothly from one line to the next.

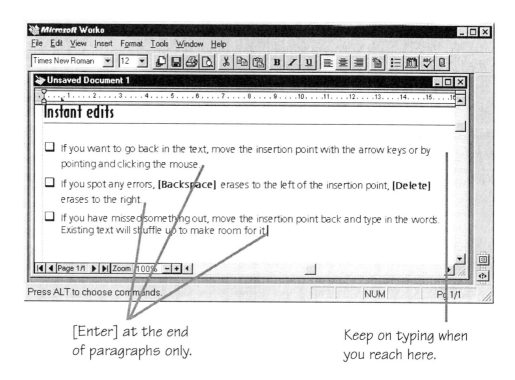

[Enter] at the end
of paragraphs only.

Keep on typing when
you reach here.

Instant edits

> If you want to go back in the text, move the insertion point with the arrow keys or by pointing and clicking the mouse.

> If you spot any errors, **[Backspace]** erases to the left of the insertion point, **[Delete]** erases to the right.

> If you have missed something out, move the insertion point back and type in the words. Existing text shuffles up to make room for it.

How to select text

Text can be selected with the keys, but it is simplest to do it with the mouse. To select...

a block: Click to place the insertion point at the start. Hold down the button and drag to the end.

a word: Place the insertion point in it and double-click.

all the text: Open the **Edit** menu and choose **Select All**.

A block can be any size from one character to the whole document.

Click here...   ... and drag to here to select

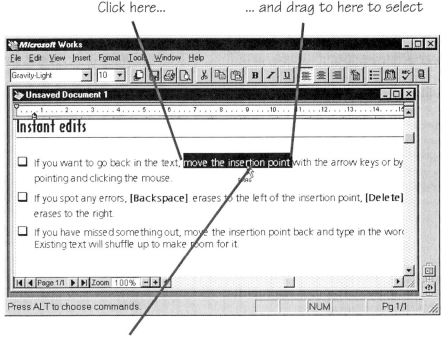

Drag on a selected block to move it to a new place.

Once you have selected a block of text, you can:

If you hold [Ctrl] when you drag, the block is copied, not moved.

➤ **apply a font style or paragraph format** – using the toolbar buttons or the Format menu

➤ **delete it**. Press **[Backspace]** or **[Delete]**

➤ **move it**. Point at the block, hold down the left button and drag. You will see MOVE beside the pointer. Release the button to drop the text into place.

How to set fonts and styles

Font styles can be applied in two different ways.

➢ Set them at any point, to apply to everything you type afterwards – until you change them again.

➢ Select a block, **anywhere in the middle of the text,** and apply a format to that block only.

All aspects of the text can be set through the **Format Font and Style panel**, but if you are changing one feature only, it is quicker to use the toolbar buttons.

Pull down the list to change the Font from the toolbar – the built-in samples will help you to choose a suitable one.

Bold Italic Underline

The font was changed when the insertion point was here – before typing the next paragraphs.

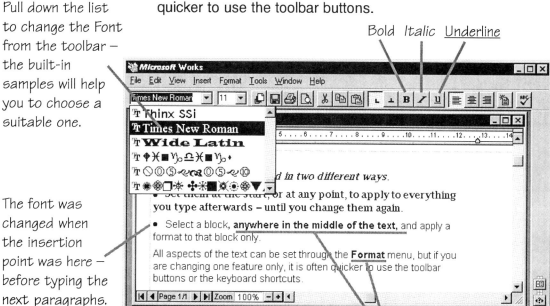

These blocks were selected and then formatted.

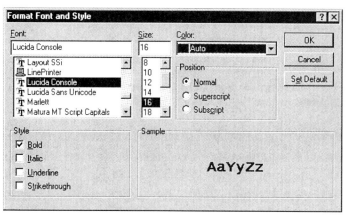

Use the menu command Format > Font and Style to open this panel.

How to indent text

Indents and alignment are both ways of controlling how the text sits in relation to the left and right margins.

Indents push the text in from the margins. There are three indent settings:

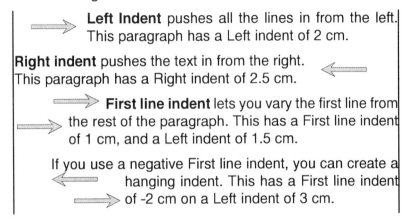

Left Indent pushes all the lines in from the left. This paragraph has a Left indent of 2 cm.

Right indent pushes the text in from the right. This paragraph has a Right indent of 2.5 cm.

First line indent lets you vary the first line from the rest of the paragraph. This has a First line indent of 1 cm, and a Left indent of 1.5 cm.

If you use a negative First line indent, you can create a hanging indent. This has a First line indent of -2 cm on a Left indent of 3 cm.

To set indents

➢ Select the paragraph(s).

➢ Drag the indent markers along the Ruler. Set the Left indent before the First line – the two are linked.

If you can't see the Ruler, use View > Ruler to turn on the display.

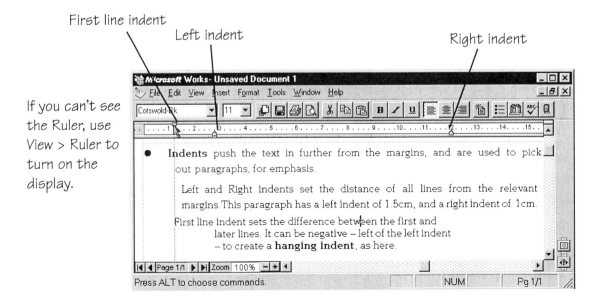

First line indent

Left indent

Right indent

How to align text

Alignment refers to how text lines up with the margins (or indents if they are used).

Left ▤ alignment is the default. Lines start flush on the left, but have ragged right edges.	**Fully justified** ▤ text aligns with both margins. This gives a crisp right edge, but can produce big gaps between words.	**Centre** ▤ alignment is good for titles and special effects, but does not make for easy reading.	Use **Right** ▤ alignment for addresses, dates and other headings.

To align Left, Right or Centre

➢ Select the paragraph(s).

➢ Click a toolbar button.

How to add buttons to the Toolbar

If the Justified button is not on the Toolbar, add it like this.

Find the Justified button and drag it up onto the Toolbar.

Use Tools > Customize Toolbar... to open this panel.

Click on Format in the Categories list.

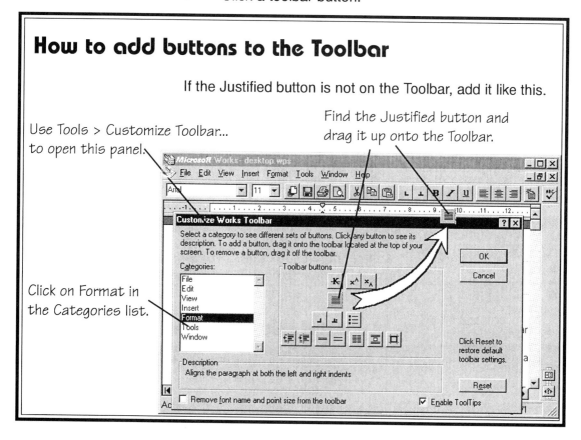

The Format Paragraphs panel

This handles Indents, Alignments and the Spacing between paragraphs. Use **Format > Paragraph** to open the panel.

To set indents accurately

Type in the Indent values, or use the arrow buttons to nudge the values up or down.

The Windows 3.1 version also has a Quick Formats tab on this panel.

You can set the Justified alignment from this panel.

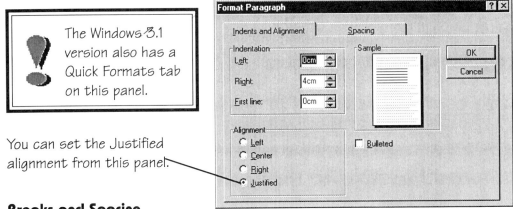

Breaks and Spacing

Spacing can be set to single-line and double-spacing using the Toolbar buttons. For accurate spacing between lines and Before and After paragraphs, type the values into this panel.

How to create templates

If you have a document which you want to reuse with new text in future – e.g. headed paper – you can save it as a template. When you open the **Save As** dialog box, click the **Template** button to open this panel and type in a name. The document can be reopened later from the Wizards panel (or the Templates panel in the Windows 3.1 version).

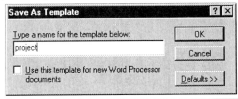

How to set margins

Before you get too far into typing the text, you should check that the basic layout of the page is right. Use the **Page Setup** routine to set the margins.

The sample gives you a rough idea of how it will look. Use File > Print Preview or View > Page Layout for a better idea of how your printed page will appear.

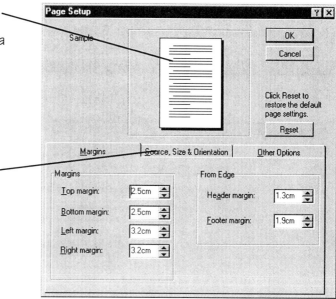

Paper Size and Orientation can be set from the second tab on this panel.

The Header and Top margins must be at least 5 mm apart – to allow room for one line of Header.

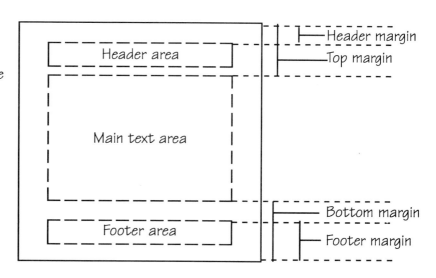

The Bottom and Footer margins can be the same – but will look better with a few mm of space.

How to add borders and shading

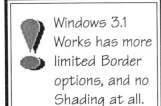

Windows 3.1 Works has more limited Border options, and no Shading at all.

Borders can be used to make attractive title pages, or to focus attention on a block of text. The block can be any number of paragraphs – there is a whole page option in Windows 95 – and the border lines can go on any or all sides of the block.

Works for Windows 95 users can also add shading.

Lines all around create a solid box. This can work well around the title on the front page of a report.

Use lines above or below paragraphs to mark sections.

Lines on either side can help to emphasise a block of text. If you also Indent from both sides, it will help to pick out the block.

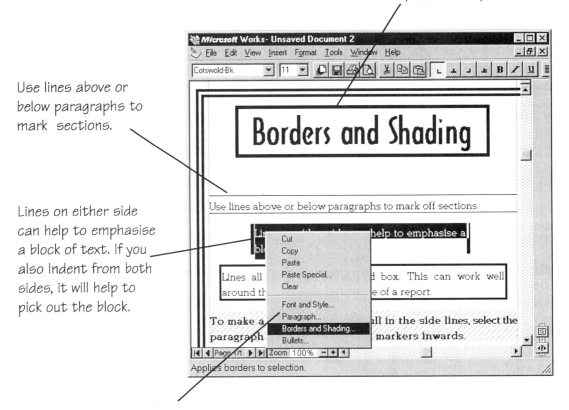

Click the right mouse button over a selected paragraph to get its short menu. You can reach the Borders and Shading settings from this.

Select Border side(s) first, ticking those to have lines, then select the line style.

If you have selected a set of paragraphs, *Top* and *Bottom* put lines by each separate one; *Outline* surrounds the whole set.

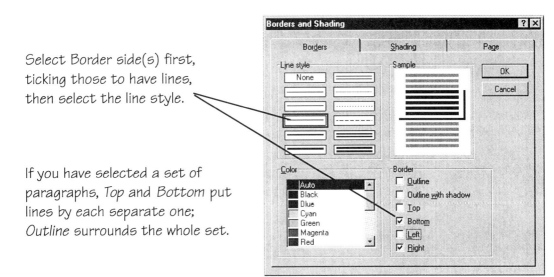

Use the Page tab to put a border on a whole page.

This can be set for *first page only*, if you just want it for your title page.

If you change the *Distance from page edge*, you may have to change the Margins in Page Setup.

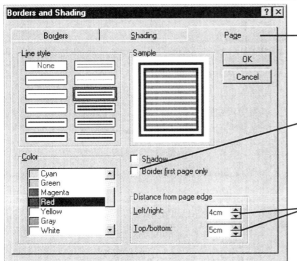

Solid shading with contrasting text makes a paragraph leap out at the reader, though patterned backgrounds can make text more difficult to read.

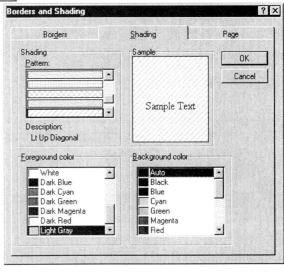

How to use Easy Text

Easy Text is Works' way of automating typing. Use it for common phrases or sentences – standard openings or closures to letters, client's addresses, long product names, or whatever. After you have typed the text once, you call it up again with a couple of mouse clicks.

Creating Easy Text

You can type the text when you get into the Easy Text system, but if you have already written it in your document, highlight it before going into New Easy Text. When you get to the dialog box, you will find your text is in place, and all you have to do is give it a name.

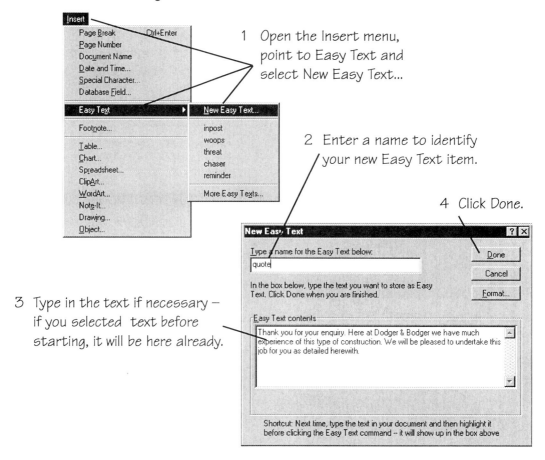

1 Open the Insert menu, point to Easy Text and select New Easy Text...

2 Enter a name to identify your new Easy Text item.

4 Click Done.

3 Type in the text if necessary – if you selected text before starting, it will be here already.

Using Easy Text

If you just have a few items of Easy Text, you can pick them off the **Insert > Easy Text** menu. This lists only the first five.

If you have lots of Easy Text items, you can reach the rest through the **More Easy Text** option. This takes you to the main Easy Text control panel. (You can also get here with the **Edit > Easy Text** command.)

Select an item and click Insert to place the text at the current point in your document.

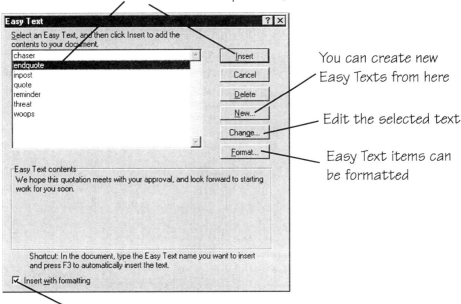

You can create new Easy Texts from here

Edit the selected text

Easy Text items can be formatted

If you don't want the Easy Text's formatting, switch it off before you click Insert.

Level 3 – Automated Routines

Works for Windows 3.1 cannot handle Easy Texts, macros or any other form of automation.

The nearest it can get is Find and Replace (next page). This lets you replace an abbreviation with a full phrase or paragraph, as often as required, throughout a document.

How to find and replace

Find

This will track down a word or phrase. Use it to check documents for references to particular items, when you do not know if they are there or not. You can also use it to jump to a part of the document identified by a key word. The longer the document, the more useful this becomes.

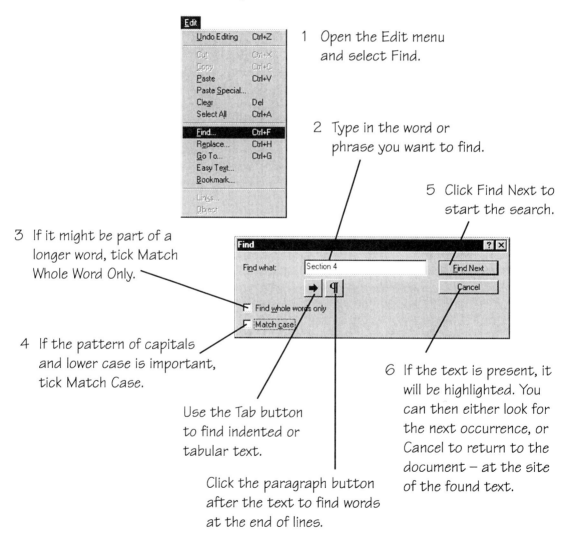

1 Open the Edit menu and select Find.

2 Type in the word or phrase you want to find.

5 Click Find Next to start the search.

3 If it might be part of a longer word, tick Match Whole Word Only.

4 If the pattern of capitals and lower case is important, tick Match Case.

Use the Tab button to find indented or tabular text.

Click the paragraph button after the text to find words at the end of lines.

6 If the text is present, it will be highlighted. You can then either look for the next occurrence, or Cancel to return to the document – at the site of the found text.

Replace

This will find the given text and replace it with a new phrase. it is said that some unscrupulous authors use this to make new books from old. A quick Replace on the names of the key characters and the places, and you have a fresh novel!

It is more commonly used as a time-saver. If you had a long name, such as "Butterworth-Heinemann", that had to be written several times in a document, you could type an abbreviation, "B-H", and later use Replace to swap the full name back in.

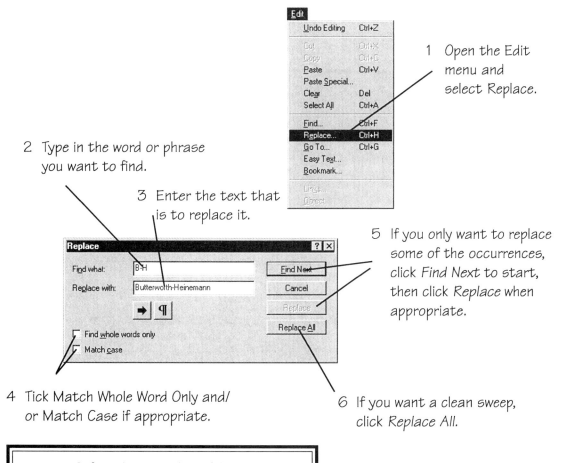

1 Open the Edit menu and select Replace.

2 Type in the word or phrase you want to find.

3 Enter the text that is to replace it.

5 If you only want to replace some of the occurrences, click *Find Next* to start, then click *Replace* when appropriate.

4 Tick Match Whole Word Only and/ or Match Case if appropriate.

6 If you want a clean sweep, click *Replace All*.

Before doing Replace All on a short word, check both the Match options. There is a chance the word could be found as *part* of another word – and you won't want that replacing!

How to spell check

Even the best spellers need these! You may not make spelling mistakes, but is your typing perfect?

The spelling checker has a dictionary of over 100,000 words. It's a good number, but it won't include all the words that you use. Specialised terms and names of people and places are the most likely omissions. To cope with these, there is a user dictionary, to which you can add your own selection of words. Once added, they will be included in spelling checks in future.

1 The check will normally run through the whole document. If you only want to check a single word, or a block of text, select it first.

2 Start the spell check from the Tools menu or click on the Toolbar.

3 When an unknown word is found, it is highlighted and this dialog box opens.

Replace with the word in the Change To slot – you can edit this first if you want.

It's OK, leave it...

... every time you see it

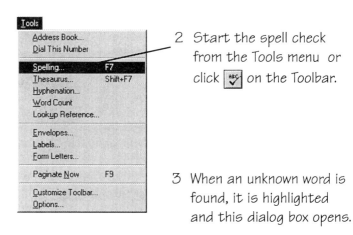

Replace with this word every time

Brings up a list of possibilities – likely ones are suggested automatically.

Add to your personal dictionary

How to print

Before you print anything for the first time, you should check the settings – adjusting if necessary – and check its appearance through Print Preview.

1 Use File > Print to open this panel.

2 How many copies?

If you have printed the document before, AND you know all the settings are right, AND you want all the pages, just click 🖨

3 Select All, or the range of pages to print.

6 Print if you are happy with the preview.

4 Use Draft quality for rough copies – it's quicker.

5 Click to Preview the printout.

Use the magnifying glass to Zoom in for a closer look.

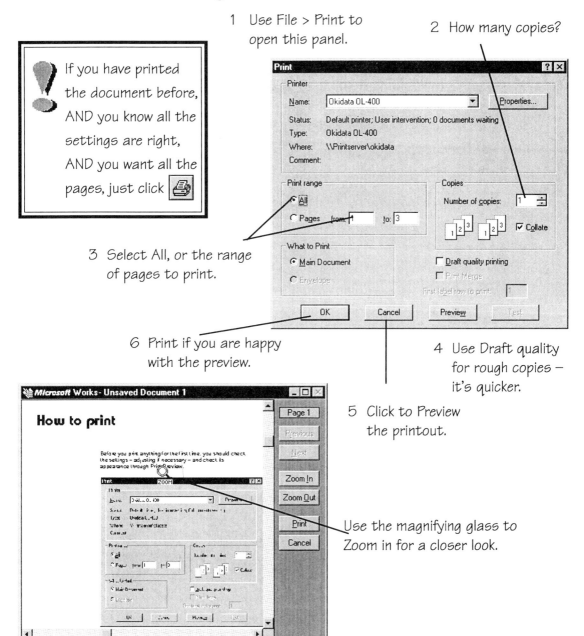

How to import graphics

The ClipArt Gallery supplied with Works contains around 300 images – there should be something here to meet most situations!

1 Use the Insert > ClipArt command to open the ClipArt Gallery.

3 Scroll through the thumbnails and select an image.

4 Click Insert.

2 Select a category.

6 Type a word that you might expect to be in the Description.

5 If you are not sure which category to look in, click Find...

7 Click Find Now and insert an image from the found set.

How to format objects

You can adjust is size and position of a ClipArt graphic – or any other object – to fit in with your text.

To **resize**, click on the object to select it, then point at a side or corner handle and drag to resize.

If you want the object to be next to, or surrounded by, your text, use the **Format > Text Wrap** command and switch from **In-line** to **Absolute** mode.

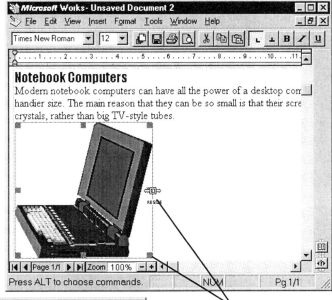

When first inserted, the object will be In-line (i.e. on a line by itself). You can use the Alignment options to set it to the Left, Center or Right.

In Absolute Text Wrap mode, you can place graphics next to text.

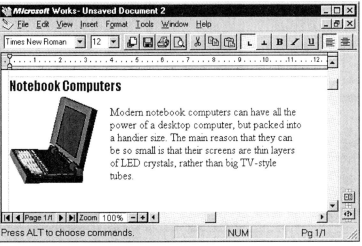

If you drag a corner handle, the object keeps its proportions. The side handles adjust the width and height separately.

How to import a spreadsheet

There are several ways to import a spreadsheet into a word processor document.

> If you want to insert a table, or other named range, from an existing spreadsheet, open it in Works, switch back to the word processor and use the **Insert > Spreadsheet** command.

> If you want the whole of an existing spreadsheet, use **Insert > Object**, taking the **Create from File** option.

> If the spreadsheet has not been created yet, use **Insert > Object**, and take the **Create a new** spreadsheet option.

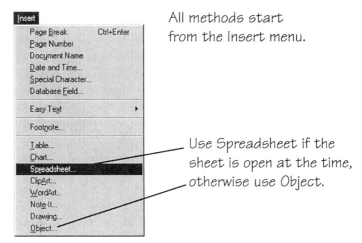

All methods start
from the Insert menu.

Use Spreadsheet if the
sheet is open at the time,
otherwise use Object.

Select the sheet, and then
the range, to be inserted.

See How to use
names, in the
next chapter

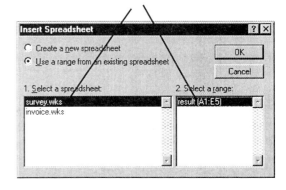

To create a new spreadsheet for insertion, highlight Sheet in the list, select Create New and click OK.

If it exists, use Create from File and click OK, then Browse for the file.

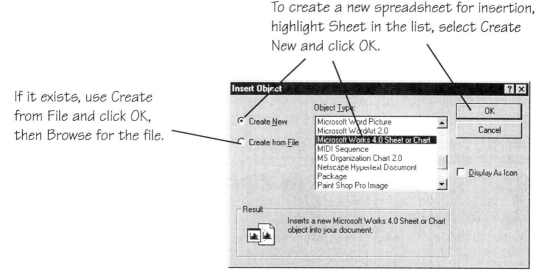

To edit or format the sheet, double-click on it to open the spreadsheet window.

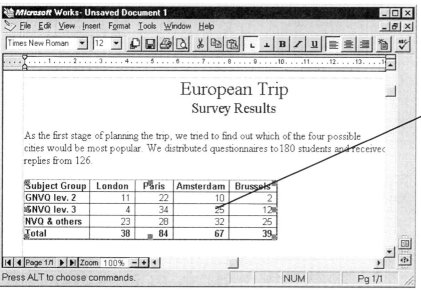

Formatting the spreadsheet

Use **Format > Text Wrap** or the alignment options to set the spreadsheet's position.

To change the font, size or style of text, or to add borders or colour, open up the spreadsheet window and reformat there.

You can resize the sheet by dragging, but you will get a better-looking result if you adjust the font and cell sizes within the spreadsheet window.

How to merge files

Merging word processed files is just a matter of Cut and Paste. Formatted text can be copied just as well from one document to another, as it can within a document.

Four commands are needed:

Windows > Tile arranges the open documents side by side in the window.

Edit > Select All selects all the text of a document.

Edit > Copy copies the selection into the Clipboard.

Edit > Paste pastes the Clipboard's contents at the current insertion point.

The Clipboard is part of Windows. It is where copied material is stored.

1 Open both files and Tile the display so that you can reach them both easily.

3 Use Edit > Copy to copy it into the Clipboard.

2 Go to the document to be imported and highlight it all with Edit > Select All.

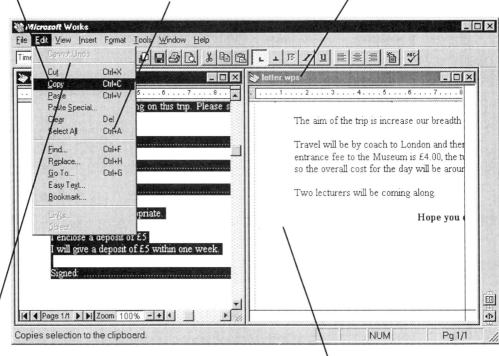

5 Use Edit > Paste to paste in the formatted text.

4 Go to the 'master' file and place the cursor where you want the new text to go.

Works Spreadsheet

11

How to enter and edit data

Entering data into a spreadsheet is significantly different from entering it into a word processor. Everything goes in through the Formula line, where the system checks it to see if it is text, a number or a formula – these are all treated differently. The Formula line is linked to the current cell. It displays whatever is in the cell at the moment, and anything entered into the Formula line is transferred to the cell.

3 Use the arrow keys to move along the line; [Backspace] or [Delete] to erase errors.

2 Enter and edit data here.

1 Click on a cell to make it current.

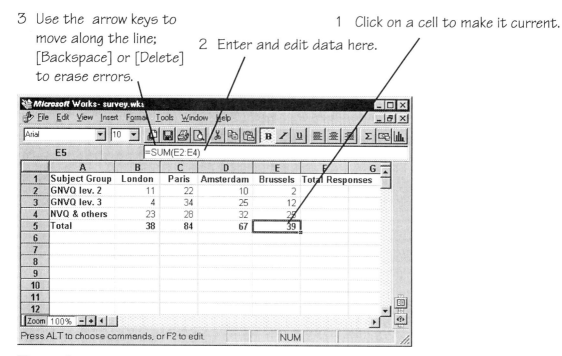

Two layers

Spreadsheets work on two layers – the contents and the display. The text, numbers and formulae that are held in the cells are not necessarily what you see on screen.

➢ With formulae, the results are displayed.

➢ Text items longer than the width of the cell are clipped short if there is something in the cell to the right.

➢ Numbers appear as ####### if they are too large to fit in a cell.

105

Files and directories

The Help Pages

Word Processor

Spreadsheet

Database

Column letters

Wide text will flow over into empty cells

Formula line

Fonts and Formats

The current cell or range reference is shown here

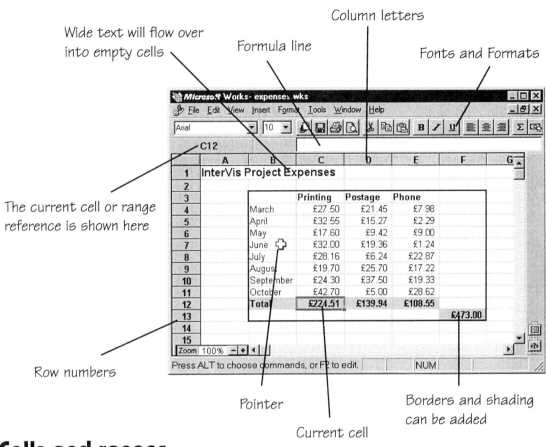

Row numbers

Pointer

Current cell

Borders and shading can be added

Cells and ranges

Each cell is identified by a **cell reference** – a Column letter/ Row number combination. In the illustration, the current cell is C12 (Column C, Row 12).

A **range** is a set of cells, which may be one or more full rows or columns, or a block in the middle of the sheet. To select

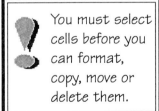

You must select cells before you can format, copy, move or delete them.

➤ a block – drag the mouse pointer from one corner to the opposite one

➤ a row – click on the row number

➤ a set or rows – drag down the numbers

➤ a column – click on the column letter

➤ a set of columns – drag across the column letters.

How to format numbers

The way in which we write a number depends upon what it represents. If it is money, we would write a £ sign before and show two figures after the decimal point; with a large number, we would put commas every three digits to make it easier to read; if it is a percent, we place a % sign after it.

Works knows about all this. It can display numbers in different formats, and can understand numbers that are written in different formats. Type in £12,345.67 and it will realise that the underlying number is 12345.67, and also that you want to display it as currency. Type in 50% and it will store it as 0.5, while showing 50% on screen. Type in 0181-123 4567 and it will not be fooled into thinking that it is a sum – this gets treated as text. Try it and see for yourself.

The Formats

General is the default – numbers appear as they were written

Currency places a £ at the front, commas every 3 digits, and normally 2 decimal places: £1,234,567.89

Comma places a comma every 3 digits: 12,345,678

Percent multiplies the value by 100 and adds the % sign at the end: 50%

Exponential is used for very large or very small numbers: 2.34500E+05

Fractions can sometimes be useful. Let it work out the closest fraction, or fix the denominator

Text treats the digits as text, not as a value.

107

Files and directories

The Help Pages

Word Processor

Spreadsheet

Database

1 First select the range of cells to be formatted.

2 Open the Format menu and select Number.

4 Set the number of decimal places.

5 With *Currency*, you can display Negative numbers in red.

7 Click OK.

3 Select a Format from the panel.

6 Check the Sample and adjust the options as required.

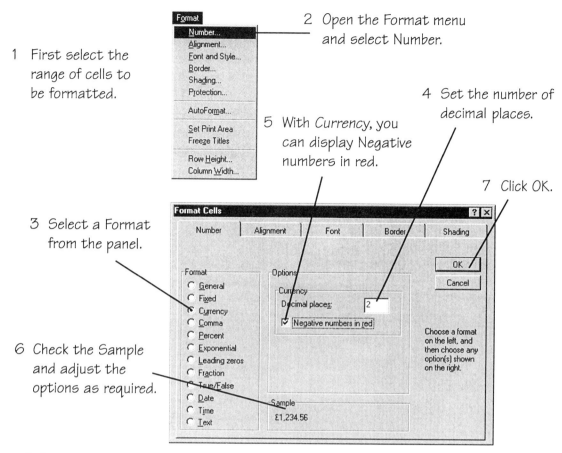

Below is a small selection of the number formats. The number of decimal places can be set in any format. With Currency and Comma formats, negative numbers can be shown in red.

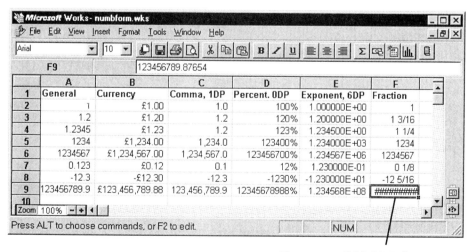

	A	B	C	D	E	F
1	General	Currency	Comma, 1DP	Percent. 0DP	Exponent, 6DP	Fraction
2	1	£1.00	1.0	100%	1.000000E+00	1
3	1.2	£1.20	1.2	120%	1.200000E+00	1 3/16
4	1.2345	£1.23	1.2	123%	1.234500E+00	1 1/4
5	1234	£1,234.00	1,234.0	123400%	1.234000E+03	1234
6	1234567	£1,234,567.00	1,234,567.0	123456700%	1.234567E+06	1234567
7	0.123	£0.12	0.1	12%	1.230000E-01	0 1/8
8	-12.3	-£12.30	-12.3	-1230%	-1.230000E+01	-12 5/16
9	123456789.9	£123,456,789.88	123,456,789.9	12345678988%	1.234568E+08	#########

If you see "######" increase the column width to display the number properly.

How to set fonts and styles

The simplest way to set one aspect of the text is to select the cell or range and click a toolbar button.

2 Pick from a drop-down list...

1 Select the cells.

3 ... or click a button.

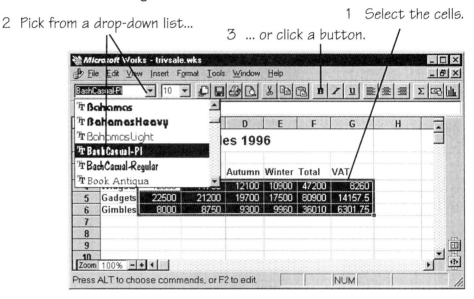

If you want to do a real make-over – setting alignment, borders and other aspects as well as Font and Style – right click on the selected cells and use the **Format** option to open the Format panel.

You can switch to other tabs to set the Alignment, Borders, etc. for the selected cells.

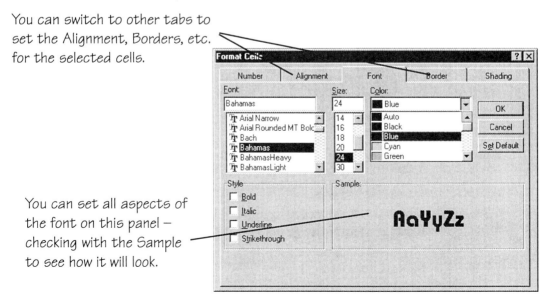

You can set all aspects of the font on this panel – checking with the Sample to see how it will look.

How to use alignment

There are more alignment options in the spreadsheet than in the word processor. As well as **Left**, **Right** and **Center**, you have:

➢ **Fill,** which fills a set of cells with the character(s) in the leftmost cell.

➢ **Center across selection**, which sets the text in the leftmost cell in the centre of a set of cells.

➢ **General**, which aligns text to the left and numbers to the right. This works well, though the headings of columns of numbers look better if they too are aligned to the right.

➢ **Vertical** alignments – allowing you to position text or numbers at the Top, Center or Bottom of the cells.

➢ **Wrap text** packs long items into several lines within a cell, rather than letting them sprawl across to the next.

"Sales 1996" is in A1, but has been centred across the set A1:G1. It is also centred vertically.

Wrap text turned on for this note.

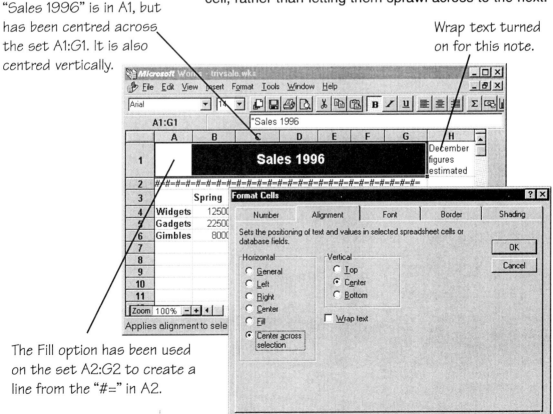

The Fill option has been used on the set A2:G2 to create a line from the "#=" in A2.

How to add borders

Borders can help to create a visual structure for your sheet. Placed around a block, they will group the contents into one unit; placed along one side or beneath, they will separate values from their headings or totals.

Set the line style and colour before selecting the sides if you want all the borders to be the same. If you want varied lines, set the styles before ticking the each required border.

1 Select the cells to be formatted.

BUG ALERT! You cannot remove a border from the Outside of a block, by setting none for the Outside . You must set none for *Top, Bottom, Left* and *Right*.

2 Open the Format menu and select Border...

3 Select the Line style, and Color if wanted.

4 Click on the Borders which are to be lined.

5 Click OK.

Outside applies to the whole block only.

Top, Bottom, Left and Right apply to each cell within a block.

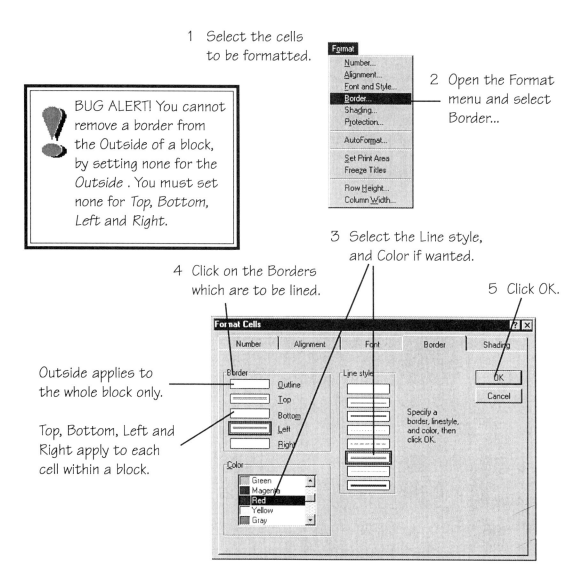

How to add shading

Shaded and coloured backgrounds can focus your readers' attention on the most important aspects of the sheet – though some patterns can make the contents virtually unreadable. This may, or may not, be a bad thing.

1 Select the cells first!

2 Open the Format menu and select Shading.

3 Pick a Pattern.

You can work through the tabs and set all aspects of format for the selected cells.

4 Set Foreground and Background colours

For coloured text, use the Color option in the Font panel.

5 When you are happy with the Sample, click OK.

Patterns can make the contents unreadable.

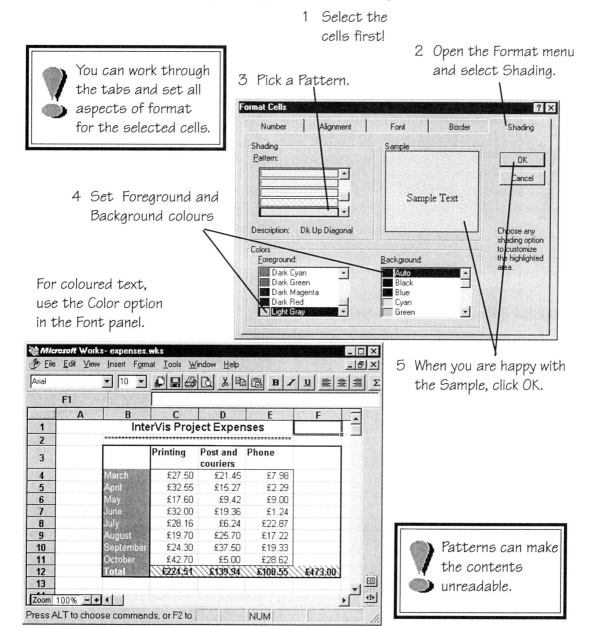

How to copy cells

The usual **Edit Copy**, **Cut** and **Paste** facilities are available in the spreadsheet, as anywhere else in Windows, but there are also alternatives which may be better.

Much of your copying is likely to be of formulae to create a table. For this, the **Fill Right** and **Fill Down** commands are quicker and simpler. They will take the formula in the first cell of a range and copy it into all the other cells, adjusting the references as they go, so that the formulae continue to apply to the same relative cells.

For example, if you had a formula in C2 that read:

=A2+B2

When this is copied down into C3, the formula will read:

=A3+B3

As you would normally want the same type of formula all down the table, this automatic adjustment of references is generally a good thing.

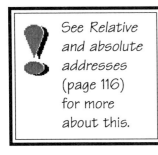

See Relative and absolute addresses (page 116) for more about this.

1 *Write a formula in the cell at the top of the table.*

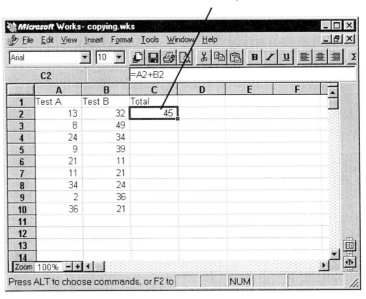

2 Select the range, starting with your formula cell and continuing to the bottom of the table.

3 Open the Edit menu and select Fill Down.

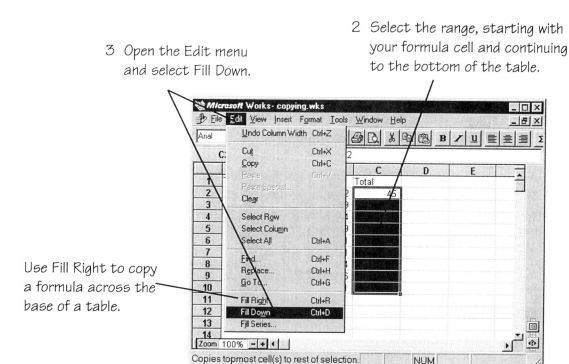

Use Fill Right to copy a formula across the base of a table.

4 Check any of the new formulae and you should see that their references have been adjusted to suit their new positions.

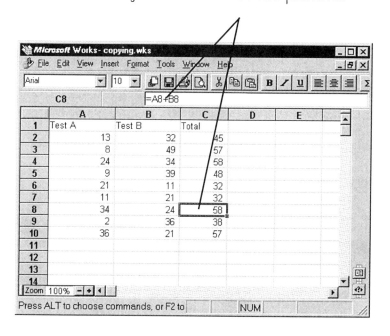

How to move blocks

The spreadsheet layout is not fixed. At any point you can move, insert or delete rows or columns, or move blocks of cells. Whole rows and columns are easy to move.

Columns are moved in the same way. Look for the DRAG arrow by the right of the column.

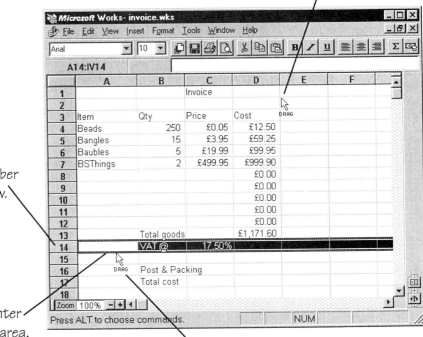

1 Click on the number to select the row.

2 Move the pointer into the grid area, near the bottom of the row.

3 When the pointer changes from the cross to the DRAG arrow, hold down the mouse button and move the row to its new place.

4 Release the button and the row will insert itself between the existing rows.

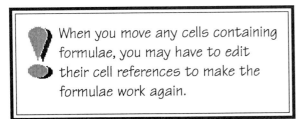

When you move any cells containing formulae, you may have to edit their cell references to make the formulae work again.

Blocks within the sheet

Think hard – and save the file – before you move a block of cells within the sheet. It can be dangerous.

When you move a full row or column into a new position, existing lines make space for it, and the hole that it left is closed up. When you move a block, you lift its data and formulae out of the cells and place them in the new location. A hole is left behind, and the moved contents will overwrite anything that was there before.

3 Drag the outline to its new position, taking care not to overlap any wanted data.

2 Place the cross pointer over any of the edges or corners to get the DRAG arrow.

1 Select the block.

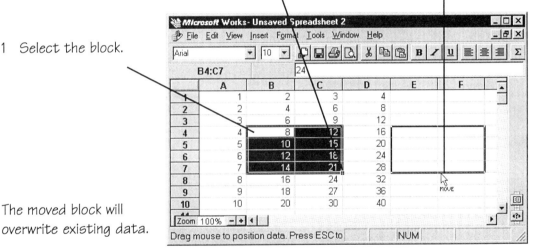

The moved block will overwrite existing data.

4 Release to drop the block into its new position.

 If a move goes wrong, you can use Edit – Undo to restore the sheet to how it was before. This will only work as long as you haven't done any other editing after the move.

Relative and absolute addresses

In "How to copy cells" we noted that the system normally adjusts any references when copying a formula. Sometimes you will want to copy a formula, but keep a reference unchanged.

➤ **Relative addresses** are adjusted when they are copied.

➤ **Absolute addresses** remain the same when copied.

In the example here, the VAT formulae (column G) have references to the Totals (column F), which must be changed, and to the VAT rate (in B10) which should stay the same.

To keep a reference unchanged, edit the formula and type a $ sign before the column letter and row number.

G4 held this:

=F4*B10

when copied into G5 it reads:

=F5*B10

This cell's address must not be changed when the formula is copied.

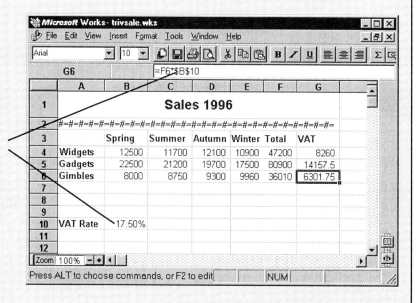

How to use names

Cell and range references are hard to remember, and if you reorganise the layout of the spreadsheet, you may have to learn them all again. To make life simpler, Works allows you to give meaningful names to cells and ranges. Use them – they will make your formulae more readable.

1 Select the cell or the range.

2 Open the Insert menu and select Range Name.

If a range is to be inserted into a word processed document, it needs a name.

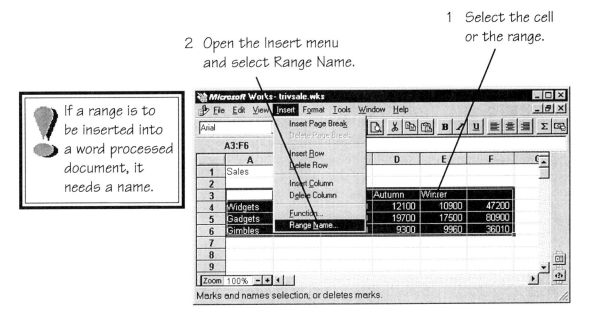

3 Type a suitable name into the top slot.

4 Click OK.

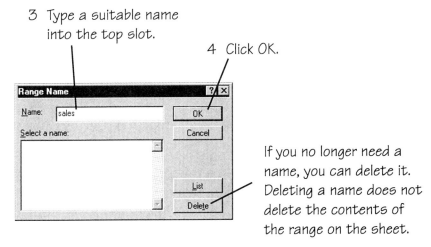

If you no longer need a name, you can delete it. Deleting a name does not delete the contents of the range on the sheet.

How to print

Before you print, make sure that the printer is set up correctly for your output, and that the sheet layout and formatting will work on paper.

File > Page Setup

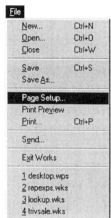

The key decision here is whether to print the normal way up – Portrait – or with the paper on its side – Landscape. If the occupied area on your sheet is wider than it is high, Landscape printing will make better use of the paper.

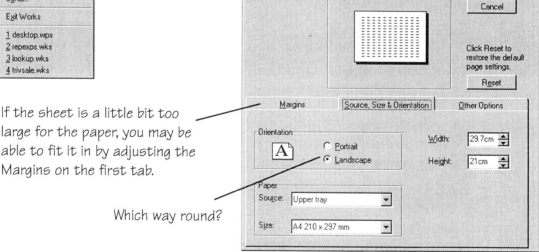

If the sheet is a little bit too large for the paper, you may be able to fit it in by adjusting the Margins on the first tab.

Which way round?

File > Print Preview

Use this to check the appearance of the hardcopy before you print – it will save you time and paper! After previewing, you may want to go back to Page Setup and change the Orientation or Margins. You might even want to go back to the sheet and change some Shading patterns or Fonts. Things that work well on a colour screen do not always look so good in black and white!

File > Print

Before you click OK, consider:

➢ Do you have a choice of **printer**?

➢ Do you want to print **All** of the sheet, or selected **pages**? (See below)

➢ Is this the final copy, or a quick printout for checking? **Draft quality** printing is faster and uses less ink, but is good enough for you to be able to see it clearly.

➢ Do you want more than one copy? If you do, and there are several pages to print, turn **Collate** OFF for faster printing; leave it ON to have the pages ready sorted.

Which printer?

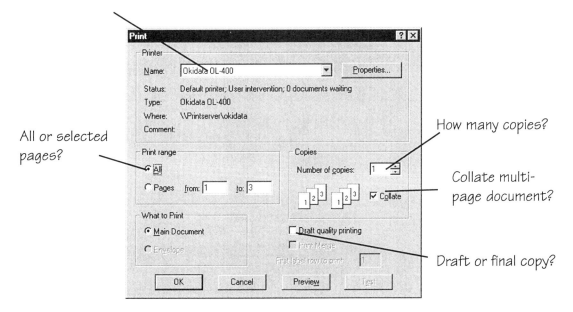

All or selected pages?

How many copies?

Collate multi-page document?

Draft or final copy?

How to print part of a sheet

Works spreadsheet does not let you select an area to print. You can print all of it, or selected pages. If you just want to print one area of a busy sheet, insert rows and columns around it so that, when printed, it will be on a page by itself.

To insert rows or columns, select the row numbers or column letters where you want the new lines, and use the **Row** or **Column** option on the **Insert** menu. Existing rows will be moved down; existing columns moved to the right.

How to write formulae

Works makes writing formulae a fairly painless business. If you want to total a column or row of figures, it only takes a click of a button with **Autosum**. Other calculations take a little more effort, but point and click references and lists of functions simplify the process and reduce errors.

A formula starts with the = sign and can contain a mixture of cell or range references, numbers, text and functions, joined by operators. These include the arithmetic symbols /*-+^ and a few others.

Examples of simple formulae:

=4*C1	4 times the contents of cell C1
=B3+B4	the value in B3 added to that in B4
=SUM(A5:A12)	the sum of the values in cells A5 to A12.

References can be typed into the formula line, or pulled in by clicking on a cell or highlighting a range.

4 If range covers the right cells, press [Enter] to accept the formula.

2 Click on the Autosum tool.

3 You will see that the column (or row) is highlighted, and that there is =SUM(range) in the formula line.

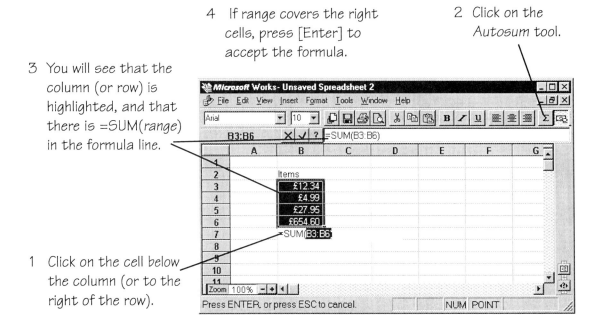

1 Click on the cell below the column (or to the right of the row).

How to display formulae

If you want to check formulae – or prove that they exist – you can set the display to formulae, rather than their results.

Printing

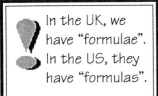

In the UK, we have "formulae". In the US, they have "formulas".

The printout follows the screen display, so if **Formulas** are turned on, that's what you get. Works automatically makes columns wider when displaying formulae. Before printing, you might want to shrink the columns to get a better, more compact, layout.

Open the View menu and tick Formulas.

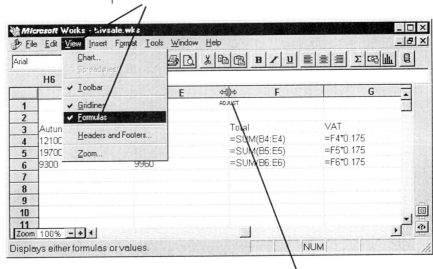

Shrink over-wide columns by dragging the dividing line to the left.

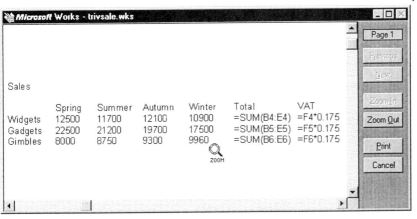

How to create graphs

Graphs and charts can bring out the underlying patterns in sets of numbers, and with Works you have a good range of charting styles to cope with all kinds of data. Creating a chart could scarcely be simpler, and once created, a chart can easily be adapted. A few minutes' experimenting with different styles should be enough to find one that best displays the underlying patterns.

To create a chart, you must have a table of figures. Works assumes that the table has headings above and to the left, and that the data is organised with the series in rows.

If your table is organised any other way, you will need to use the Advanced options.

 A set of figures forming one line on a graph, or one set of bars on a chart, is called a series.

1 Select the table of cells containing the figures and their headings.

2 Open the Tools menu and select Create New Chart... or click the Chart tool.

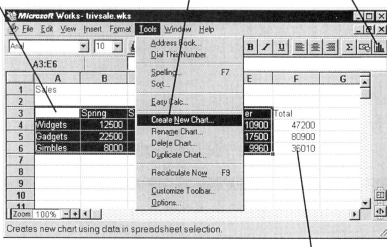

Don't include Totals in your graphs!

If you have several charts on one sheet, or if you want to insert charts later into a word processed document, give them meaningful names with Tools – Name Chart.

3 Pick the Type – this can be changed later, if necessary.

5 If your table is non-standard, open the Advanced Options tab.

4 Add a Title, Border and Gridlines if wanted.

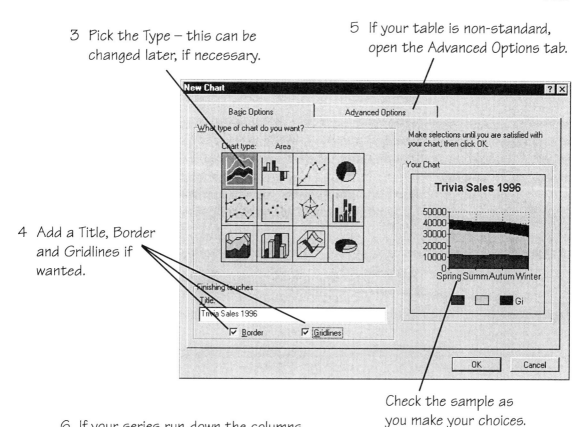

Check the sample as you make your choices.

6 If your series run down the columns, click on the Down option.

7 If the First column does not contain headings, click on Category.

8 If the First row does not contain headings, click on Y values.

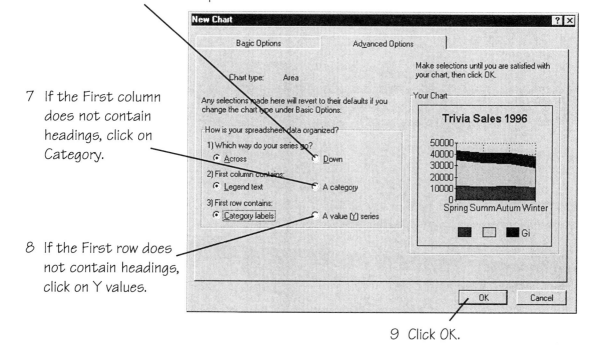

9 Click OK.

How to make a template

When you save a sheet based on a template, give it a new name – if you don't change the name, you'll mess up the template.

There is no magic to spreadsheet templates. A template is simply a sheet with all its text, formulae, formatting and other permanent fixtures – but without any actual values. Common uses for templates include invoices, estimates, budgets and similar jobs where you want to perform the same sets of calculations regularly, but using different values each time.

➤ Set up the sheet, and enter (simple) numbers so that you can check that all the formulae are correct.

➤ Remove the test numbers and save the sheet. You have created a template.

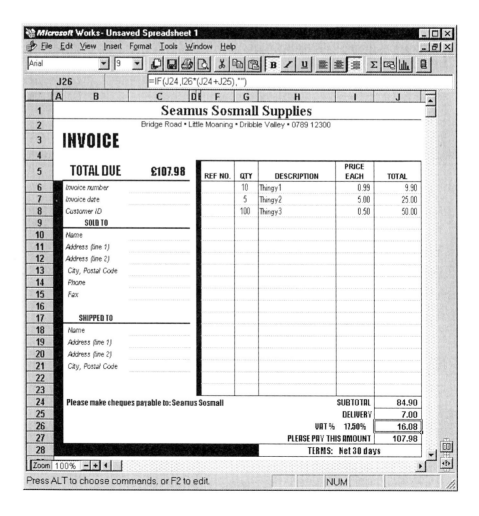

Works Database

How to create a database

Plan the structure of your database, and write down the names and formats of the fields it will have. Take a sample of your data and check that it will fit into your structure. Does it work? Yes, then it's time to put it into Works.

1 Start up Works, or open the File menu and select New.

2 Go to Works Tools and click on Database.

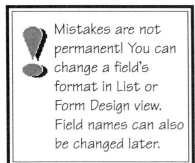

Mistakes are not permanent! You can change a field's format in List or Form Design view. Field names can also be changed later.

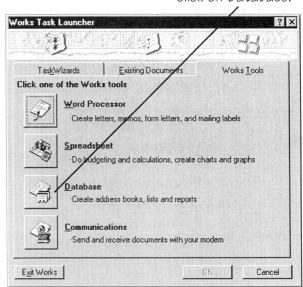

3 Type the Fieldname for your first field.

5 Click Add.

4 Set a suitable Format.

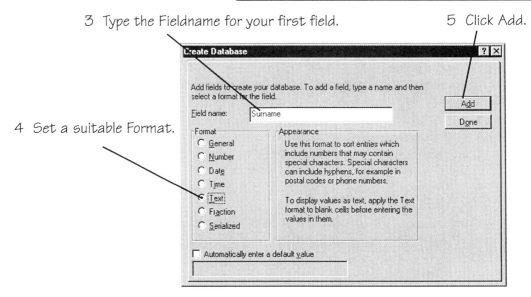

6 Repeat for all fields, then click Done.

With *Date, Time* and *Number* formats, select an Appearance.

If you want ID numbers on your records, include a Serialized field. This numbers each new record as you create it.

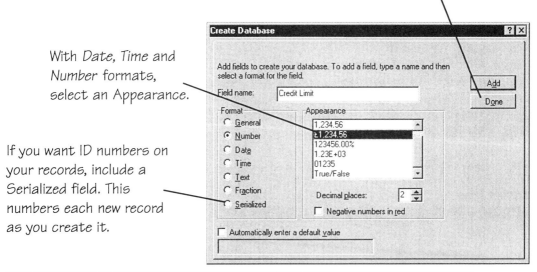

The new database opens in List view. You may want to switch to Form view for easier data entry. (See page 128.)

Before you have done too much work on the database, save it!

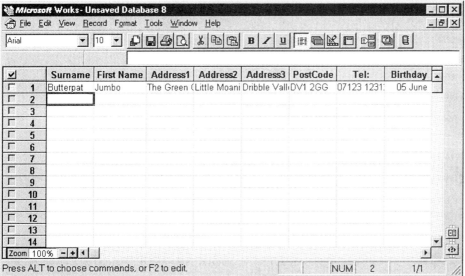

How to enter and edit data

You can work with the database in either List or Form view.

Using form view

The Form view is generally the best one for entering and editing data. You normally work on one record at a time, this view shows all its details. You can move between fields and between adjacent records, either with the mouse or with these keys:

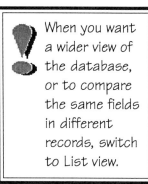

When you want a wider view of the database, or to compare the same fields in different records, switch to List view.

[Tab]	next field
[Shift]+[Tab]	previous field
[Ctrl]+[PgDn]	next record
[Ctrl]+[PgUp]	previous record
[Ctrl]+[Home]	first record
[Ctrl]+[End]	last record

3 Press [F2] or click the cursor into the text in the entry line.

Click to switch to List view.

4 When you have done, press [Enter] to accept the changes, [Escape] to leave it unchanged.

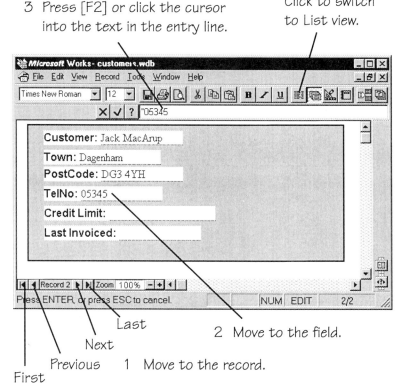

Last

Next

2 Move to the field.

Previous   1 Move to the record.

First

129

Files and directories

The Help Pages

Word Processor

Spreadsheet

Database

List view

This view looks like a spreadsheet. You can see a screenful of records at a time, though some of the fields may be off the sides. It is useful when you want to check, or edit, the values in one field throughout the database, and it is simpler to hunt for records when you can see 15 or 20 at a time.

Enter and edit data just as you would in the spreadsheet. (See page 104.)

Formatting and adjusting the table are much the same as in the spreadsheet, except:

> **Fonts, borders and shading** cannot be applied to a single cell or block. They always apply to whole fields.

> **Insert Record** ⊞ **Delete Record** ⊠ and **Insert Field** ⊞ have buttons. There is no button for **Delete Field** as they don't want to make this too easy. Use **Record – Delete Field**, or delete it in *Form Design view*.

> You can adjust the heights of records and the widths of fields, and note that the changes you make here are not carried over into the Form view.

In Form Design view, you can format, move or resize fields. You can also add extra text for headings and decorative rectangles.

There are no Format options on the short menu in List view. Use the Format menu if you want to reformat fields.

Click to go to Form view

Click to go to Design Form view

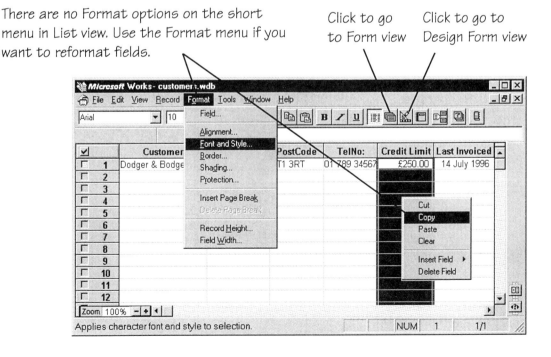

How to create filters

If you want to find a record, or pick out a set of records that share some common values, then you must create a **Filter**. In this you define what value, or range of values, you are looking for in a particular field. At the simplest you might look for the person with the surname "Jones", or pick out all those customers whose debts were over their credit limits.

For the first of these, you would search the *Customer* field, using the comparison "is equal to" with the value "Jones".

For the second example, you would search the *Amount Owing* field, using the comparison "is greater than" and comparing it to the *Credit Limit* field.

If you want to get more complicated, you might set up a filter to find, for example, those clients in Manchester who do not owe money and haven't received a visit from the rep in the last month.

After you have applied a filter, only those records that match are displayed.

> Filters are saved with the database and can be reused. It may take a while to set up a filter to pick out the right records, but you only have to do it once.

The examples shown here are based on this set of records.

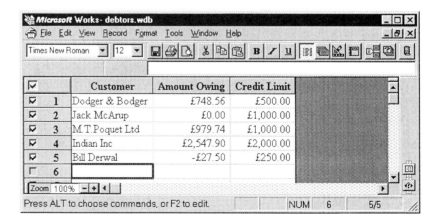

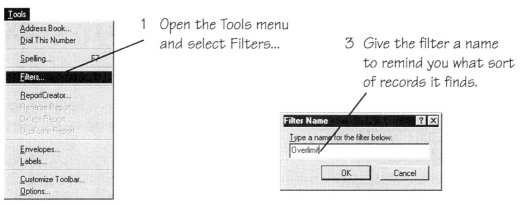

1 Open the Tools menu and select Filters...

3 Give the filter a name to remind you what sort of records it finds.

4 From the Field name list, pick the field that contains the values you are looking for.

Existing filters can be selected from this list.

5 Pull down the Comparison list and pick an operator.

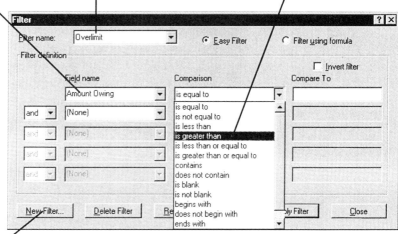

2 Click New Filter... – you won't need to for your very first filter.

6 Type a value or a field name into the Compare To slot.

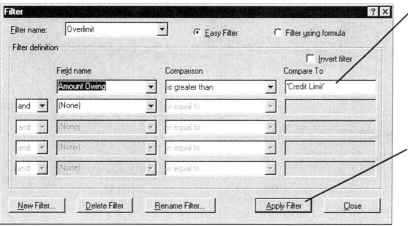

7 Click Apply Filter.

How to design a report

The database's report routines produce lists of the data held in the records. You have a little control over the layout, but full control of the content. You can:

➢ select the fields to be included in the reports

➢ sort and group on one or more fields

➢ restrict the report to filtered records

➢ include a variety of summary statistics.

Designing a report is not difficult, but it takes a little time to work through all the tabs. Just keep setting options and clicking **Next>** until you reach the end!

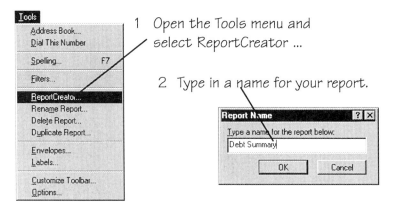

1 Open the Tools menu and select ReportCreator ...

2 Type in a name for your report.

3 On the Title tab, check and edit the basic layout – title, orientation and font.

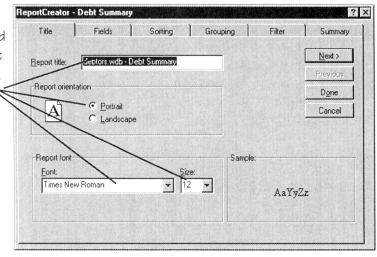

4 On the Fields tab, select the field to be included and click Add> after each.

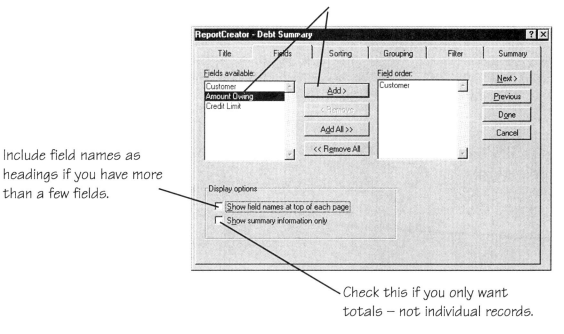

Include field names as headings if you have more than a few fields.

Check this if you only want totals – not individual records.

5 On the Sorting tab, if you want the output sorted, select a field to Sort by and set Ascending or Descending order.

Use multiple sorts where you have a lot of records – e.g. a club database might be sorted by category of member, sex, then alphabetically by surname.

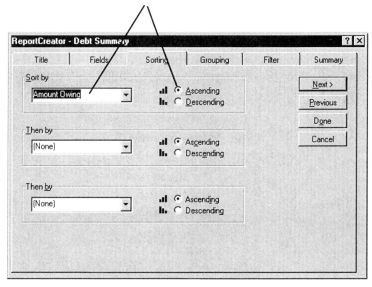

6 On the Grouping tab, if you have set a *Sort by* field, you can also opt to group on this field. Use this where records may have the same value in the *Sort by* field, e.g. Town.

When records are grouped, you can have a heading and a new page for each group.

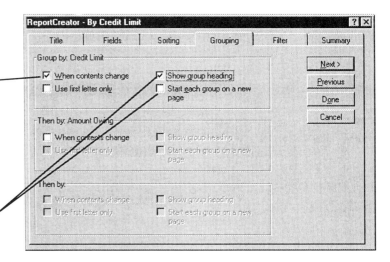

7 On the Filter tab, select the set of records to be output. These can be all records, the current displayed set or those from a filter.

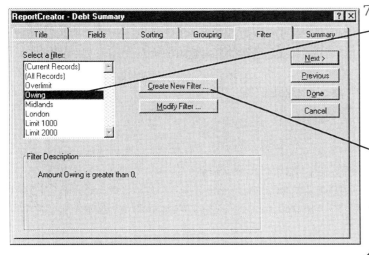

You can create a new filter while you are on this tab.

8 On the Summary tab, select a field for which you want one or more summary figures.

9 Tick the Summaries you want for that field.

10 Repeat 8 and 9 as required.

With Grouped reports, Summaries can be printed after each group, or all together at the end.

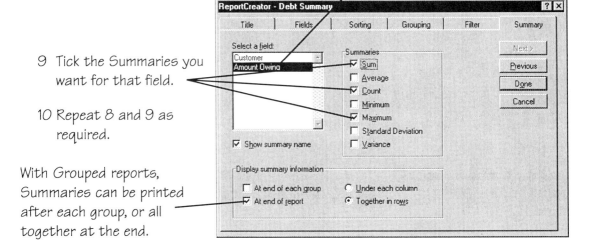

How to improve the printout

When the report is complete, you will be offered a preview. Use it – it will be your first chance to see what it looks like.

Needs Currency format, and something to say what it is!

Could be bigger

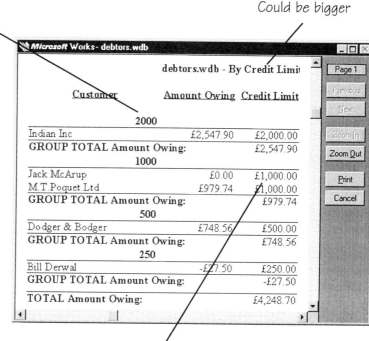

We don't need the Credit limit here as well as at the start of each group

If you do not like the appearance, you can adjust it in Report view. Editing and formatting here is similar to that used on the spreadsheet – but not quite the same.

➢ Titles, headings and any other simple text can be edited as normal – and you can add new text in blank cells.

➢ Text and number formats, borders and shading, column width and row heights are all the same as in the spreadsheet.

➢ If you want to move cells, you *cannot* drag them to a new position. Use Cut and Paste – but keep items in their original rows or you will ruin the output.

HANDLE WITH CARE! Save the file before restructuring. If it goes wrong, you can re-open the file to get back to where you were.

Items starting with = are pulled in, or calculated from, the database. You can delete those that you decide you don't really need, but it may be quicker and easier to redeisgn the report than to try to edit them.

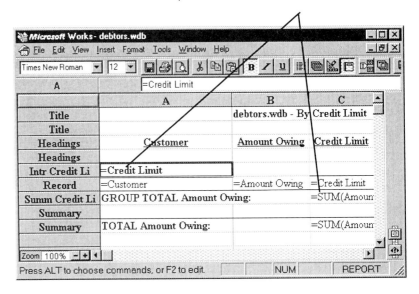

Preview again after you have edited the layout

Index